A WACKY HIPPIE TRAIL ADVENTURE

MARK A. TESORIERO

A catalogue record of this book is available from
the National Library of Australia

First Published in 2021

Copyright © Mark A. Tesoriero 2020

All Rights reserved. No part of this publication may be reproduced, stored in a retrieval system, or transmitted in any form by any means, electronic, mechanical, photocopy, recording, or otherwise, without the prior permission of the publisher, except as provided for by Australian Copyright law.

Paperback ISBN: 978-0-6450290-0-0

Ebook ISBN: 978-0-6450290-1-7

Published by: Surfer's Enterprises Pty Ltd, 2021

PO Box 1370 Manly NSW 1655

All inquiries should be made to the author:

Email: *mark_tesoriero@mac.com*

www.bombom.com.au

Bom Bom - A Wacky Hippie Trail Adventure

Non Fiction, Memoirs, Travel

Illustrations: Paul Gearside

Editor: Bruce Elder

A True Story
Mark A. Tesoriero

The Left Hand Gun

Illustrations by Paul Gearside

..A YOUNGER..HANDSOMER ME —GUNNA.

Paul 'Gunna' Gearside, animator, art director, storyboard artist, illustrator and former front-man of 70's Sydney punk band, the 'Psycho Surgeons'.

Gunna's story is really another trip, a bit more eccentric these days. Beach-combing, fishing and guitar taking up most of his time. He hadn't been drawing for a while 'til he read Bom Bom, then he was hooked!

So with a blank canvas, no pressure and free rein to put forward whatever ideas and scribbles he thought would fit the tone of my story, he delivered what we both think will give you a pretty good idea of what was '*a Wacky Hippie Trail Adventure*'.

Thank you Gunna, every picture is a thousand words!

In memory of my mate
Patrice Guilbert,
a very funny Frenchie,
a great water-colour artist,
and a wonderful man.

The stories in this book are best recollections of a time, when it was possible that reality had become fiction, or perhaps fiction had become reality. Heady days.
To protect the innocent I've changed their names.

I'd like to acknowledge the references to music and other events to give context of the time.

Thanks Pedro and Hugo for the huge memory prompts, and to our mates who kept the Mail to prove it really happened.

Lots of us have tales.
Now to tell mine.

Contents

Chapter 1   Age of Aquarius   1

Chapter 2   Stone Free   13

Chapter 3   Get Your Motor Running   25

Chapter 4   Dweller On The Threshold   53

Chapter 5   In Walked Luck   119

Chapter 6   Let The Good Times Roll   143

Chapter 7   Welcome Home   153

Chapter 8   Blowing In The Wind   159

Chapter 9   Well It's Alright   185

Chapter 10   He Told Us Not To Blow It   197

The Stoner's Glossary   205

CHAPTER ONE

Age of Aquarius

I was born into the golden age of baby boomers – the 1950s – and grew up on Sydney's lower north shore. Life was simple but not without its challenges as my parents struggled to build a home and acquire the must-have modern appliances of the time. Our extended family included dozens of cousins which was typical of Italian communities. About six of them were around my age. Outside of school was mostly unsupervised so we made our own entertainment visiting friends and playing in the local bush, creeks and river. Our push bikes were the link to each new adventure including pocket money delivering newspapers and telegrams.

It was the Beatles who turned me on to music in 1964. I saw all their movies at the local theatre and knew the words to all their songs. I think my first live concert experience was Little Pattie singing at the local shopping mall, where I joined the older kids dancing to the Stomp. Later my cousins and I got to the Pop Spectaculars at the old Trocadero – it used to stand where the current Hoyts debacle is at Town Hall station. These were great concerts – Zoot, Sherbet, Ted Mulry Gang, John Paul Young – they dressed up in crazy costumes and sang jingle songs and everyone danced.

The innocence of childhood took a twist in High School as I was one of the Italian wogs and a dago, but once the Yugoslavs turned up, the heat was thankfully passed to them. Together, and with the rest of the class, the teachers lashed us with the strap as part of some daily routine. They certainly got our attention but the punishment questioned every aspect of my Christian upbringing.

By a stroke of luck our art teacher taught silk-screen and the mono image of Jimi Hendrix's head became a T-shirt favourite. It got me interested in his music very early. I tried to mimic Jimi with the hair to some success but I was too intimidated by his riffs to learn to play guitar. When I wasn't doing school sport, I was building push bikes, billy carts and skateboards from rubbish-tip findings. I also really loved saloon car racing, and would often, unbeknown to my parents, jump a train on a Sunday and go to Warwick Farm to see my heroes risk life and limb.

When I was old enough I got my licence and thankfully had the cash from my part time jobs to swap the school bus for a trail bike. All was going well until the teachers caught my mate Paul and I pulling wheelies in the street at lunchtime. As a result the bikes were banned but, undeterred, we'd park them down the road in a mate's yard, where we could also smoke a cigarette without getting busted.

I graduated in 1972 at the height of the Age of Aquarius. A sense of awareness and freedom had permeated society. My dad swapped the Brylcreamed short back and sides for an over-the-collar look and my mum wore a kaftan. My four brothers and

I had lots of hair and were into surf, skateboards, pushies and motor bikes. Life was driven by great music, unforgettable lyrics, free love and an optimism that has since been lost to the world.

Times were a-changin. After twenty-three years of conservative government Australia decided It's Time and voted in Gough Whitlam and his Labor Party. This set in motion a number of radical social and economic policies that would result in free university, free healthcare and ultimately the end of Australia's involvement in the Vietnam War. Thank God someone had the sense to stop sending Aussie kids to be killed in someone else's debacle.

Sex, dope and rock'n'roll were the mantra of the day. And there was plenty to go round. Given I'd been to an all-boys school I was still finding my way around the girls, but I was enjoying smoking pot which I'd been doing it since I was fourteen, and hadn't yet turned into the crazy guy from the *Reefer Madness* movie. The music of the time came from traditional record shops and the rare stuff from Anthem Records which was one of the first "import" stores. 2SM and 2UW owned AM pop radio and the real rock'n'roll was on an ABC-TV program called *GTK,* which aired every week night. I even managed to get to a few *GTK* recordings (*Max Merritt & the Meteors, Jeff St John and Spectrum*) at the old ABC Studio when it was under the TV tower at Gore Hill.

So, with school behind us, my best mate Pedro and I, loaded up our trail bikes and headed north to easy-ride our way to hippie-town Nimbin and beyond. It started off a bit rough when about one hundred kilometres out, Pedro ran up the back of a Vee Dub Beetle that had suddenly stopped and his Honda left knobbly tyre marks all the way to the roof. It was a really heavy thing, but very funny to watch as Pedro and his bike stood motionless on top of the car for a few seconds, before leaning sideways and tumbling off. Thankfully Pedro only suffered a few grazes. So we dusted off his bike and polished out the rubber marks on the Dub. He apologised heaps and on we pushed.

It was amazing how far we went as "heads" on the north coast of New South Wales. The bush was full of alternative beings living and smoking the dream. There was always a place to crash, a meal on offer, or bounty to be picked from farmlands or the bush.

It was here we wrestled our bikes through hundreds of miles of amazing forest fire-trails and tried our hand at a number of culinary techniques to make the gold top mushrooms, that we collected from the cow paddocks of the Promised Land, somewhat palatable. None of the recipes worked, but the mushrooms sure did! I remember we ate about six each and nothing happened for about an hour. In despair we went to the pub where they suddenly ignited and sent a hot flush straight to our brains. We were lucky to find the exit without being restrained. These were our first hallucinogenic trips. They lasting about six hours and, thankfully, were conducted in the quiet and safety of the beach sand hills at night. No one to see us digging *Alice in Wonderland* rabbit holes and howling at the moon.

Sharing all this with Pedro was the best part. He was about a year younger than me but like a big brother. He was about six foot tall, broad from swimming, and had shoulder length red hair and light freckled skin. Pedro had an infectious laugh to support his great sense of humour and, if he wanted, he could muster a deep voice that would scare the shit out of anyone. He was pretty academic, had a great perspective on life, and was ready to ride any wave that came his way. Music was a big part of Pedro and he spent a lot of his cash on records. He made audio cassette compiles and was always turning someone on to a new band or music style. Pedro loved his hot shots. Flaming *Southern Comfor*t was his nirvana, until one night he was pissed and missed, and set his face alight. The result: a badly singed moustache, eyebrows, eyelashes and fringe which led to lots of silly comments and laughter. Pedro loved surfing, motorbikes and adventure, and when not burnt looked like James Dean in double denim and boots.

Tripping around up the coast was a fantastic escape, and the ocean-front camping was awesome. At one point we camped on Aboriginal land, met the locals and got some depressing insights into life on a "reservation". Overall the whole Aboriginal experience was, and still is, a pretty shameful exercise on white man's part. With limited cash we soon returned to Sydney to find our way into a career and further education.

I was lucky to get an advertising cadetship and started a course at East Sydney Tech at night, and Pedro signed up for an Arts degree at Sydney Uni. It was free! We were having a carefree time but the scene was very small, the grog was getting tiresome, and we yearned for greater adventure. We were also very silly eighteen and nineteen-year-old boys and if we didn't change our surroundings there was a good chance we'd get into some real trouble. Nothing criminal like, but it was before Responsible Service of Alcohol and Random Breath Testing and there were some very narrow escapes. Fortunately, we were able to spend a lot of our spare time riding off steam around a bush or race-track and got close to God that way.

A few of our friends weren't so lucky. One tried to push his car over a cliff for the insurance and went with it. One fell from a party balcony and impaled himself on the fence below. Another got hit by a car while changing a flat on the side of the road. And one got mixed up with Mr Asia and ended up dead from a heroin overdose. All very sad. We really hadn't had to deal with the Grim-Reaper up until then, but with this wave of friendly corpses it became a scary reality that reinforced our need to do everything we possibly could before Doctor Death came a knocking.

We had a little motorcycle and Hendrix-lovers group called the Woof Brothers. Our motto was "ride hard, die free". We would meet regularly to party. Our school mate Marcus hosted a lot of the time. His oldies were really cool. He had lots of brothers and sisters and they all had friends and their rambling house easily accommodated loud music and group sleep overs.

We loved our motorbikes, riding hard, and testing our mettle. Lots of other guys and girls were doing the same so we made heaps of new friends and tried to earn their respect by trashing their favourite street-circuit times. A couple of unlucky ones ended up in hospital. And amazingly no one was killed, but it was our dirt-bike buddies with whom we had the most amount of fun.

Some of these friends were renting an old market-farm on the outskirts of Sydney. We were there for a three-day party and *Goat's Head Soup* was playing on high rotation. There was plenty of grass, some interesting girls and a guy who had just returned from travelling in India. His stories were wild and intriguing. Out of this world. At one point Pedro and I caught each other's eye. There was a raise of the eyebrow and a glint that without a word sealed the deal. We were going to check this out!

At the next opportunity I quit my job to start a higher paying labouring job at the fruit markets. Pedro postponed uni and got his bartending "degree" and as many shifts as he could at the local hotel. I often waited for him after closing time as he hosed out the tiled floor of a bar that would easily sit fifty guys. Public bars were tough places in those days and the women waited outside.

We gave ourselves twelve months to stash away as much as we could. As soon as we had the first $320 we went to the steam-liner company and bought our ticket. There was no turning back.

We were going to the U.K. which was a rite of passage in those days. A lot of my older cousins had done it, got work, tripped around Europe and come back with that badge of honour. We were going to do the same, but instead, we were going to do the overland trip home through India and the "Mystical East".

We really had no idea what was ahead of us as we both still lived at home. Pedro lived in his oldies garage and I converted our under-house storage into a pretty neat bedroom, complete with day-glow posters, a black light and record player. I was listening to my older brothers' music until my first purchase of *Are you Experienced* and *Deep Purple in Rock*. We had some independence from our parents but they still knew when we had a friend over or were "burning hay" late into the night.

The twelve months couldn't have gone quick enough, even though we were having a whole lot of fun. The Australian Rock'n'Roll music scene was right up there with AC/DC, The Angels, Midnight Oil, Billy Thorpe and a dozen other world class acts bashing it out on the pub circuit of Sydney. Pubs were a great breeding ground for talent, helped along by the fact that there was one on every corner. The Antler at Narrabeen, the Manly Vale Hotel, the Bondi Lifesaver and the Coogee Bay Hotel were the great music venues of the day.

The Arts Factory in Sydney was also a favourite haunt and Tully a favourite band. It was at one of these gigs that my cousin Johnny and I heard about the Pilgrimage for Pop, the first outdoor music festival in Australia, at rural Ourimbah a few hours north of Sydney. Keen to get our dose of Woodstock we were among the first to hitch our way out there. It was a funny scene, very bluesy. Some known bands like Tamam Shud, The Nutwood Rug Band, Max Merritt, Jeff St John and Doug Parkinson grooved it out, and other experimental musicians got the chance to do their thing.

We took acid, got our clothes off, swam in the river and met new people who exposed us to some wild ideas and experiences. It was mind blowing to see just how left field some people were, and it certainly made us look like "fresh meat". Tripping on acid was interesting. I'm not sure what the dose was like, but it was a lot milder than the mushrooms. It came on pretty quickly, there was an amazing clarity and sensitivity to everything, and you just floated along. Soaking in the warmth of the sun and the music was a great experience and like most hallucinogens it was great sharing with friends.

With a huge appetite for live music, Australia was starting to become an important stop on the world tour for some big international acts. We got to see some golden moments like Black Sabbath at the old Showground Hordern Pavilion, and The Rolling Stones rocking up at Randwick Race Course in the Queen's gold carriage drawn by six white horses. At the time there were very few venues capable of holding more than a few thousand people, so music popped up in some strange places. The Stones concert was particularly crazy with about twenty thousand fans standing on the horse track, all lighting up to create a cloud of smoke that would have stoned three neighbourhoods. We pre-rolled joints and inscribed each with a song title that became a salute to the music when played. Funnily, at the end of the night the only joint left was *Soul Survivor*.

Our next "Woodstock" was the Aquarius Festival in Canberra. It was another 'hippies are happening' event and, as it was really, really hot, clothes were optional. I don't remember much about the music but there were lots of joints, a great river and the girls were very exciting.

The next big three-day music festival was Odyssey at rural Wallacia on the Australia Day long weekend. It was promoted and hosted by a cat named Adrian Rawlins who also MC'd the Pilgrimage for Pop and was Om-ing on stage at Aquarius. He was a larger than life, poetry reading, arty type who you'd swear was always tripping. He was always laughing and would often chuckle and bellow without stop. He had no inhibitions so was very funny, and I remember later seeing him on GTK just laughing for the full five minutes of the show.

I travelled out to Odyssey with Johnny in his friend Zac's old Chrysler ambulance. His "Ghostbusteresque" ambo always got the looks. It was no different that day when we drove up to the gate to pay our entry, and the guys collecting the dough just waved us through. Before we knew it, we were parked alongside the stage. Zac got the patter down quickly, "we were there to pick up the bummers". What a great scam and what a great three days. Thankfully, we weren't called on to help any bummers, as we were in no state to even help ourselves.

Johnny and Zac were in a low-key band called The Sot Weed Factor. They had their guitars and jammed near our campsite. It was amazing how many of the paid talent dropped in to share some chords and belt out some songs. It was surreal sitting there beside my music heroes and offering up the joints.

Billy Thorpe and the Aztecs with Lobby Loyde were the act of the weekend. Billy (*"Most people I know think that I'm crazy"*) was an animal on stage – such tough rock n roll. Wendy Saddington and Copperwine were doing "Janis", and Daddy Cool were at their peak. We were also introduced to an eclectic Kiwi line up that called themselves the La De Das and whose members, lead guitar hero Kevin Borich and rhythm guitar man Phil Key, have since become a bedrock of Aussie music.

Meanwhile back in Sydney we were hanging out with another group of friends who had rented a share-house in Chatswood. We went to the Showground Speedway (daringly awesome) with them every Saturday night. They had dope growing in the backyard, a keg in the kitchen, motorbikes in the lounge room and the music was always loud. They were crazies. They even heated Castrol R motor oil to get in the mood while listening to sound-blasting audio recordings of the Isle of Man TT.

One of the guys was a ratbag Norton-riding electrician who rode flat out everywhere, often bouncing off parked cars and sliding off through corners, all the while with his bull-terrier gripping for life on a hessian bag he had thrown over the tank. They both carried the scars. Another was a huge guy called the Hulk who smoke two joints, before he smoked two joints, and then he smoked two more. He later rode a stunt bike and crashed big time in the biker movie *Stone*. Then there was Woody, a real biker with colours, a BSA and lots of leather-clad babes always hanging around. One day he came out of his room with three very sleepy and undressed girls. He was a lovely guy, loved his beer, was always laughing and was rumoured to have a huge schlong. I figured that's how he got his nickname. I was always a bit nervous when visiting these guys, as I expected the vice squad would one day bust down the doors.

I remember riding up to the Easter bike races at Bathurst with the Hulk and another guy called Rip. We got as far as Amaroo Park when Rip missed a corner and ended up tangled in a wire fence. He had broken bones so we used tie-downs to hold him upright while I pillioned him to Nepean Hospital on our way through. The four days at Bathurst was outrageous as the racers defied speed and gravity up and over the mountain while the crowd of 30,000 carried on like animals on the hill. It was the days before police presence so you can imagine the bon-fire initiations and tests of skill as the revellers burned around an amphitheatre two feet deep in beer cans and bodies. There were so many bikers in town that you couldn't find a bike park anywhere. The whole weekend could probably be surmised when riding home in a long convoy behind a dishevelled guy wearing only a hessian sugar bag with Northern Territory number plates.

When we weren't riding we were taking acid at the Yellow House art space in Potts Point where pop artists like Martin Sharp were living and modernists Brett Whitely and John Olsen were displaying their works. It was two rambling multi-story Victorian mansions connected by a hole in the wall and every room had a different theme. The sign above the ticket office said: "Price of Entry - Your Mind". Pop art, a surf movie projected on the wall, a walk-through sculpture, liquid light shows - there were some crazy people doing some very improvised art on the ceilings, walls and floors. And with music from the incredibly-voiced Jeannie Lewis it was a hip place to trip. We'd often bump into the people we met there, tripping on through Cooper Park at Bellevue Hill after all else had closed.

But, *Time waits for no one* (Mick & Keith are the Rock Lords), and before we knew it we were inoculated, getting passports, and starting to pack our bags. We really had no idea of what was going to unfold. I had five thousand dollars, Pedro had about three and half and we both expected it was enough to travel the world. There was very little travel information in those days - even about Europe. Ship and bus tour brochures were about the extent of it. No travel guides, and certainly nothing about travelling in the Middle or Far East. There were however a few newspaper articles written by Richard Neville about his overland trip to London, where he established the UK version of his counter-culture magazine *Oz*. Good info which we packed away.

CHAPTER TWO

Stone Free

July, 1974. The time had finally come. We each had a suitcase. Mine packed with loads of tees, a couple of cheese-cloth Indian shirts, AMCO baggies, and a pair of Levi's 501s which you could only get from the disposal store Surf Dive & Ski in George Street. Plus a pair of long leather boots, thongs, swimmers, a towel, a sweaty or two, a Mexican wool coat and toiletries. Something for all seasons.

A few weeks out from travel the shipping agent sent a letter upping the fare to $340, which was a $20 rise and they demanded payment before sailing. I remember the confrontation. It sounds funny now, but it was a big deal at the time and we weren't alone as we joined the queue of other unhappy passengers at the agent's Hunter Street office where we paid up and got our tickets.

It was a Woolloomooloo Wharf paper-streamer departure just like the old movie reels. A cool winter's morning and my family were there to say goodbye. It was sad but exciting to see them disappear as the ship backed out of the wharf and headed up the harbour. As Sydney Heads got smaller behind us the realisation hit - we were leaving our secure family nests, for the unknown, and we were on a ship so there was no turning back. We were in fact *Stone Free,* to do what we please.

I was going to miss my brothers. We were pretty tight. The youngest was nicknamed Tez by his surfing/skating militia. He was skating people's empty pools very early in the piece and had sessions with the Z-Boys who really pushed his style. The oldest was an events marketer for a bunch of youth brands. He set up some great surf, skate, BMX, motocross, track bike and car racing events, and brought in a lot of talent from overseas to help lift the bar. We got to hang out with a lot of them which really opened our eyes to their life outside of Oz.

One of my other brothers was into body boarding, camping, getting stoned and hotting up his old Type 3 fastback Volkswagen. It was great when it went. The last brother was a mechanic who ended up with the most awesome reggae music collection and the sound system to play it. Huge amp and speakers. I don't know how my oldies put up with him but it must have been my dad's forced love of Rasta! By then he knew all about Jah, Haile Selassie and I and I Positive Vibration.

Pedro had been reflecting as well. He had two siblings, both younger, an arty brother and a very smart sister. His mum and dad were cool but straight, they were feisty social thinkers having grown up in Balmain during the Depression. We both stood looking at the land disappearing into the distance and figured there was only one thing to do – have a drink! A toast: "May youthful folly keep us young forever".

The ship was a luxury liner named *America*, at least that was its maiden name and fit-out when it was launched in 1940. One year later she was stripped of her refinement to become America's largest troop carrier. In 1965 she was bought by the Greek shipping-line Chandris and renamed *Australis*. She was refitted to become the largest one-class liner in the world and was on her last legs when we boarded. In fact she was heading for the scrap yards of Southampton. She wasn't a total wreck, just seriously outdated.

Our cabin was about three decks down. We were sharing with two unknowns. The cabin had a port hole (thankfully), two single beds, a double decker bunk and a bathroom. It was small but clean and comfortable. As we unloaded our bags we met one of the other two guys we were sharing with. He was a young German about our age named Dirk and he was heading back to Dusseldorf to join his family. He'd been in Australia for a year, fruit picking and tripping around and was excited to be going home. He was planning to start an engineering degree.

Dirk had shoulder length brown hair and was wearing a slogan T-shirt with "Up is a nice place to be". We figured he was either a stoner or a sex fiend. Regardless, an instant friendship. The three of us headed out to explore the ship. When we got back we met our final cabin companion. He was a straight, overweight guy, very quiet and never looked you in the eye. He spent most of the voyage with a blanket pulled up over his head to avoid any contact. Very strange dude. Pedro called him the Big Leprechaun.

There were lots of girls on the boat heading to Mother England to work as a teacher, nurse, secretary or whatever. A few used the 'Big Market' opportunity to really blossom and subsequently became leaders in music and fashion. A couple of girls we met were acquaintances of school friends and they invited us to look them up in London.

Getting laid on the ship was easy as a lot of girls expressed their newfound freedom. We found out what Dirk's T-shirt was all about as he whored himself around. Sharing a cabin with him and his noisy friends became a challenge on a number of occasions. Dirk also became quite partial to "sucking on a scoobie" and was always hassling to get stoned.

Ship life had its routine, but we were able to mix it up thanks to some Mullumbimby Gold we carried on in our luggage. They were fairly lax with outbound security in those days and even more so in the transit ports along the way.

The crew were mostly Middle-Eastern or Indian. Nice people. We put out the good vibes and they made our trip very comfortable. Unfortunately, the Greeks who ran the ship treated them like shit.

The food was included in the fare, which turned out to be a really good deal. There was a buffet breakfast (when we weren't sleeping off a big night), a hot lunch, and you could dress for dinner. If you were lucky you got a turn on the Captain's table where you had champagne and treats. Overall the food was pretty good. Plenty of it. But the best part was that beers and smokes were duty free, and cheap. If I recall, a can of Aussie beer was just twenty five cents. Needless to say we were never thirsty, and a typical shout would mean filling the bath in our cabin with cans for a late night social.

On an average day you'd have a run around the deck, a swim, sun, drinks in the lounge and lazy cabin visits. While at night it was live music, more drinks, and joints on the rear deck while watching the smoke and world disappear in the ship's wash. What a vast space the ocean is and for a few nights we enjoyed a full moon over the water which was really unforgettable.

Luckily the sea was only rough once on the entire trip ... on the last leg in the Atlantic from Miami to Southampton. It's a mighty feeling - off your na nas on the bow of a ship as it crashes down and through giant waves. The voyage was four weeks in total which was more than enough. The transit ports really broke up the monotony.

Our first stop was Auckland where the ship docked for a day. We went ashore and hit a Maori pub which was a great intro to the locals - they were big boys, beer friendly but given we weren't bros we didn't hang around to make friends and ended up wandering the streets trying to keep out of patrolling cops and harm's way. At the time there were a lot of Kiwis (New Zealanders) in Sydney but not a lot of Maoris. I was glad to learn later that the New Zealand government embraced its indigenous community and set up a representative government for all.

Suva, Fiji was our second stop. This was jungle territory so we took a car around the island to see some of the sights. A lot of green and mostly a non-event. Lots of bananas and pineapples and only so many you could eat. They had a great tourist shopping district which in island style looked like a row of raised bamboo huts. The good news - it was tax free. Real tax free, not like these days where it's cheaper to buy in a department store. I bought a 35mm Nikon camera for $140 and studied the manual to make sure I was doing the right thing. I had a bag of Kodachrome that my rasta brother had given me but I never saw a shot until I came back home. It was a lot of guesswork.

The trip from Suva to Acapulco in Mexico was one of the longest stretches. Our impressions of Acapulco were imprinted way before we got there thanks to Cheech and Chong's *Acapulco Gold*. We were hanging out to see what all the fuss was about and were keen to replenish our carry-on stash. We disembarked hungry and tried to work out the difference between burritos, tortillas and tacos before tasting a few beers, and heading out along the long promenade that wrapped itself around the bay.

BOM BOM

Our ship was moored in the middle of the harbour and we could see the wharf where the long ships were ferrying passengers. It wasn't long before a young kid zeroed in on us and was handing over two newspaper cylinder-wraps of weed for a wad of the local currency. Almost immediately a couple of cops appeared about fifty metres away and started walking towards us. We figured we'd been set up so made a bee-line for the closest long ship. The cops picked up pace and so did we. We were running when we hit the crowd milling for the boats so we got down low and weaved our way in. The cops were trying to follow but luckily we snaked a few people and made it onto a boat. Lying low we were ferried away to the safety of our ship. It was deep sighs of relief as we reached the pontoon and headed up the gang-plank.

Once on board we busted open the wraps to inspect the magical mull and found it was laden with small stones to make it feel weighty. There was still a fair bit in there and later that night we concluded that it was '*bad ass weed*' just as Cheech and Chong described it. We made lots of new friends on board with the 'Gold' but were always careful when and where we lit up. The rear top deck was a frequent visit. It left no evidence.

From Mexico we headed south to Central America and Panama City. But first we had to traverse the eighty kilometre Panama Canal which was built by the Americans and opened in 1914. The French had earlier attempted to construct a sea level passage through the jungle at a cost of about $US235 million, but the sheer challenge of trying to remove the mud, and the mosquito's toll on the workforce, proved too much. When the Americans got their chance they started by draining the swamps and killing the bugs and built a lock system, which they graciously allowed a French boat to traverse for the very first time.

Our passage seemed to take forever as we moved lock by lock from the Pacific to the Atlantic Ocean. We eventually arrived in the capital where, keen to explore, we were one of the first off the boat. It was a really small town. Brightly-coloured buildings and small shops in a tropical setting. It was really hot and muggy so we ventured into a small bar to get a beer. The bar was pretty sombre and the other patrons all locals. We were definitely strangers in a strange land and we were getting the look from white eyes and dark, dark skins. There was no music or conversation and it was very uncomfortable. We gave each other the look, downed our beers, and headed back out while all the time making sure that no-one was following.

We were done with exploring, there wasn't a lot to see, and as we got close to the ship we came across a couple of guys our age with backpacks. They were clean-cut, skinny Americans who had travelled down through Central America but had been robbed of their cash and passports and couldn't go anywhere. They'd been to the cops who told them that they had better be gone by the next day. They were stranded and a long jail stay appeared to be their fate.

Pedro and I felt sorry for them and thought we could help get them onto our ship. The first thing was to make them look like they belonged. They each had a backpack so we broke their gear down and spread it amongst four or five returning ship friends. Our stowaways then followed us up the gangplank and found a sun chair by the pool. Their gear was widely distributed through our cabins so as not to alert the cabin boys.

The guys slept by the pool during the day and partied with us at night. Food was smuggled from here and there and they even attracted the attention of a few of the female passengers. They were super thankful and gifted us a bit of smoko. Local Panamanian weed which was red in colour and just one tug packed a big hit.

During one of our rear deck sessions we learnt that Mike and Steve had only just come out of college and hitch hiked their way from North Carolina on the East Coast of the States, across Georgia and Louisiana into Texas, and crossed into Mexico at Laredo. They then bussed and hitched their way down through Mexico, Guatemala, Honduras, Nicaragua and into Costa Rica where they were robbed at gun point. Somehow they managed to get across into Panama and hitched their way to Panama City. They hadn't eaten for the few days before we met them and when they saw our ship dock they dreamed they were on board, chowing down and heading home. The impression I got from their stories about Central America was that it was a shit fight. Lots of idiot armies, lots of CIA, lots of drugs and lots of fear.

After three hazy days at sea we were in Fort Lauderdale, Miami, and our stowaways just walked off the ship. It was really quite funny and so obvious as our ship friends dropped their gear onto a big pile at the bottom of the gang plank. The boys just packed it up, said their goodbyes and headed into their home customs/immigration office. We never heard from them again but I am sure with a lot of interrogation, and phone calls to their dads who were high up in the Fort Bragg military, they would have spent that night in their beds at home. Good deed done.

With only a day in Miami we were determined to do as much as we could to live the American dream. It was burgers, the beach, a department store and then time to leave. Just a quick taste that was a lot like being in Sydney.

Back on the ship and the last leg of the journey. Time for some detailed thinking about what we would do when we landed. Up until that point we were going to London and that was all the detail we had. It had also been a fairly liberal time on the ship and we came to the realisation that to make our money last, we had to minimise the alcohol and the ciggies. We wanted to abide by the Fabulous Furry Freak Brothers mantra that only dopes smoke dope, and fools drink alcohol. We didn't mind being dopes because they reckoned that times of dope and no money were definitely better than times of money and no dope. All options had to be explored.

Meanwhile the ship's purser was touting accommodation in London so we bought a week's worth at one of the cheaper options. It was still a lot of money but we figured we'd do that for a week to find our bearings and get into a campervan as soon as possible.

Next thing we knew we were in Southampton. Thankfully ship life was at an end. It was humbling sailing into Southampton and seeing the old buildings that were probably there when Captain

Cook left on his journey to discover Australia … and here it was two hundred years later. So much development in Australia but so little in Southampton. There were big hugs and well wishes to our fellow passengers and talk of meeting here and there.

Once down the gang plank, we tried to avoid the crowd by walking around the outside of the barricades and before we knew it we were lining up for the bus trip to London. No immigration or customs. Did we do something wrong? We weren't going back to find out! It was an enlightening journey up through the English towns and countryside and a time for reflection on what might lie ahead.

The hotel in Bayswater was a rip off. Such a tiny, head-ducking room, a toilet down the hall and a miserly breakfast. But it was close to the centre of London and in a pleasant leafy suburb. We immediately set out on foot and on the Tube to get our bearings. First stop was the Bank of New South Wales to exchange some traveller's cheques. The bank was very old school and really crowded. Full of Aussies and unexpectedly we ran into my cousin "Octopus" and his wife, Nell. They had been travelling around the UK in a late 1940s delivery van and told us of their caravan park in Brixton and we agreed to catch up.

We spent the next few days exploring the city's museums, buildings, shopping and nightlife areas and ventured into Earl's Court to see the second-hand campervan market. Everyone who was travelling bought and sold their vehicles there. As it turned out there was nothing worthwhile, everything looked like it had been on holiday a hundred and fifty times, so we bought the morning paper to check out the classifieds. There was an ad for a car yard with lots of campers so we ventured out on the Tube for a look. We found an almost new, olive green Commer that had only been across to Europe once, and it was the right price, so we bought that. The inside was comfortable. It had a pop up roof, you could walk through from the cabin, there was storage, the bench seats and table folded into a double bed and there was a gas stove and sink. To personalise the van we added a large Rolling Stone's tongue sticker that we bought in the Portobello Markets and christened her "Greenie" which became "Queenie". *"Come on Queenie, let's shake it, go, go, go little Queenie" (Stones).*

Many people credited Andy Warhol for the Rolling Stones tongue but it was actually designed by John Pasche, an art student under commission from Mick who paid him fifty quid. Thankfully, after it was copyrighted Pasche got a decent royalty, and he then sold the original artwork to a museum for £100,000. Talk about a great career starter!

We then went in search of, and found, a portable stereo. It was a giant thing that worked off about a dozen C-size batteries and, thankfully, the van's cigarette lighter. It was one of the best investments we ever made. We had a load of audio cassettes with us from home, and from that point were able to truck flat out everywhere.

The last day at the hotel was a relief. We couldn't wait to bunk down in our van. We ate the last of their stingy tea and single toast breakfasts and loaded up our gear. As we were heading out to the van we almost tripped over the hotel grocery delivery. Somehow a two hundred and fifty tea bag box and about five kilos of sugar made its way into our pantry. It felt fair given we had been fleeced.

We hit the open road for Wales with Jimi cranking out *Voodoo Child*. It was a short trip to test the car and its camper fit-out. The van was a manual and had plenty of torque but was very light and oversteered into the most basic corners. This trip was the start of a ten thousand kilometre journey where I really improved my driving thanks to the icy Alpine roads, the buffeting of giant trucks on the autobahns, the centre suicide passing lanes of crazy Italy, and the deadly coastal roads of Croatia.

The van turned out to be very comfortable. After a few days lounging our way through Wales we headed to Dover for the English Channel crossing and boarded a ferry to Calais. It turned out to be a grey old journey on choppy seas. I figured I could swim about fifty yards in those conditions but couldn't fathom how the Channel crossers swam the twenty-one miles.

Once on the other side we filled up with petrol but couldn't go anywhere as the starter motor had died. Not to be deterred we clutch-started it for a few days until we found a mechanic who quoted about $500 for a new one. We mulled this over for about an hour and decided to keep pushing. For three months we pushed. Or should I say Pedro pushed. He got really good at it, and I got really good at clutch starting. I could start it almost anywhere, even in a street parking space with less than a metre clearance using reverse gear.

CHAPTER THREE

Get Your Motor Running

Life in the van was good. It was surprisingly comfortable and we were in control. Pedro had a map of the world and we often laid it out and plotted our trip. Our budget for Europe was the money we had left after buying the van. We figured it would keep us on the road for about three months. We'd then sell the van when we got back to the UK and use that money for the overland trip.

Even though it was pretty close living, Pedro and I were getting on well. We had known each other most of our school life and had been close for the last five years. We'd become blood brothers playing football and on more than one occasion had picked the other up after a bike fall, a spin out, or a big night of drinking. Now that we were overseas together there was an added bond to ensure we got home safely. Neither of us wanted to face the other's mum.

With a ceremonial cup of tea, with sugar, we headed off to Dusseldorf to catch up with our ship buddy Dirk who was back living with his parents. Dirk was glad to see us. He had shorter hair and was keen for some fresh air. I think his oldies were on his case, so he grabbed his sleeping bag and we took off to the International Motorcycle Show in Cologne. We were like kids in a candy shop. The orange BMW R90S or green Ducati 750 Super Sports were my choice. Pedro had his eye on the Honda Goldwing and the Dutch Van Veen 1000cc twin rotary. Dirk was a tragic drooling over the Honda CB400.

After the show we figured we'd camp outside of the town and somehow ended up at a small community hall where, believe it or not, Rod Stewart and The Faces were playing with the original line up including Ronnie Wood! What an unbelievable concert, so intimate, so much energy. Rod and Ronnie were like two English fighting cocks with their spiky haircuts and duelling guitars. It remains one of the best live gigs I've ever seen.

Dirk then travelled with us to Amsterdam. It was beautiful coming in through the flower farms and windmills. We found a spot to park just on the outskirts. Our first stop in town was a café where we ordered coffee with 'special' brownies. We were apprehensive of what was to follow so we left before the 'special' took effect. It was a fun day giggling and joking as we wandered around the canals and alleyways, checking out the shops, looking at the tourists (the French and Italian girls really stood out) and all the while listening to street music and avoiding the bicycles and tourist groups.

Along the way Pedro scored some hash from a North African cafe. There were a lot of different ethnic communities in Amsterdam - it reflected centuries of Dutch colonialism. The society was inter-racial and respectful and the young folk were very friendly. Somehow we ended up having dinner at the home of a Dutch couple who were into the occult. It was crazy how this shit happens! We had our first Ouija board experience along with three or four of Pedro's hash joints.

After summoning up some long-lost relatives our hosts eventually sent us on our way with a small 'present' and we headed back to Dusseldorf and sadly parted with our mate Dirk. I remember saying goodbye. He was wearing the giant silver-flaked Mexican sombrero that he bought on our stopover in Acapulco. I remembered how it took up half our bloody cabin, how it made it back in one piece I'll never know. I figured it wasn't going get a lot of use in Germany except at some Engineering fraternity party or a twenty first.

With Steppenwolf blasting and Pedro belting out *Born To Be Wild* we headed south to Switzerland and into the Alps where it didn't take long before snow started hitting the windscreen. Our first snow experience! We had to stop and check it out, and with the Amsterdam present burning a hole in Pedro's pocket, we sat by the roadside, lit up, and took in the forest and mountain surrounds, all the while being peppered by the falling flakes. All very pretty but it was really getting chilly and wet so back in the van we made a nice hot cup of tea.

The next leg of the trip was amazing. We wound through the Alps trying to avoid the tolls on the mountain tunnels. A few times we had to double back because of snow and once we woke to a buried van and had to be towed out. Below the snow-line the views were amazing. We spent a few sunny days camping in the lush grazing valleys and bathing in the rivers, before snailing our way through the main Swiss cities and into Germany and Munich for Octoberfest - the world's oldest and biggest Beer and Cultural show.

We were hanging out for a hot shower so we checked into the Munich caravan park. It was a huge place and it was near full. After cleaning everything, including the van, we boiled up veggies and a cup of tea and settled into a game of cards. The caravan park was humming with urban jungle sounds and waves of foreign languages drifted past our van. After a while an English tongue came into focus and it sounded familiar. I knew that voice, and leapt out of the van to see two of our dirt bike buddies from that *'Goats Head Soup'* farmhouse outside of Sydney.

We scared the shit out of them, but they were glad to see us. They were just finishing their travels and were in Munich for a beer before flying back to the U.K.. They had two bicycles and some cassettes they wanted to offload and twenty bucks sealed the deal. It was the best purchase ever. We had some new music and our touring strategy changed. We now parked at universities close to young people and conveniences and headed out each day on the bikes. They proved perfect for Italy and France.

We got to the Beer Festival and had a ball. Big steins of liquid amber, giant pretzels, roast chicken, and big fat sausages. The atmosphere was excellent – loads of beer maidens and oom-pah-pah music. So many Aussies, and others belting the piss and going off. We were on a budget so we kept it real but we couldn't help getting carried along in the swill. After a big day out we liberated a few beer steins and put them on a makeshift mantlepiece in the van.

The next day we headed out to the Dachau concentration camp. It was so sad that we decided to give the rest of Germany a miss. We headed for Vienna.

The money that we took with us was starting to get pretty thin. We had money back in Australia and the time had come to call home and get it wired through. That evening we parked by the Danube River in Vienna just as the cash ran out. Next morning we woke to realise we were parked in a very busy centre of the city but it was a legal spot so we were staying put.

Mindful of the time difference back in Sydney we found the central post office and reverse-called home. International calls were a pretty clumsy exercise in those days. For a start they had to be booked. And international money transfers were a nightmare. Funds had to go to London first and then to a partner bank in Europe. After about three days we called to check the progress and we called again three days later. We ended up waiting ten days for the money to arrive. In the meantime we were living on black tea with sugar.

Hunger was kicking in bad and we were having all sorts of strange dreams and thoughts about handing ourselves in to the Australian Embassy, stealing food and even robbing people. Thankfully it didn't come to that. But there was a lot of drooling at the Black Forest cake and creamy delights in the windows of the Viennese cake shops. What a place to have no money. The pastries looked unbelievable. We spent our last two dollars on one.

A few nights before the money came we were hanging outside a jazz nightclub hearing strains of music when we struck up a conversation with a local girl named Anna. She learnt of our plight and before too long we were in the club and she was plying us with drinks. The band even shared a hash joint with us. Pedro and I developed a newfound respect for jazz music and we slept very well that night. Next morning at seven there was loud knocking on the van door. Fearing the traffic cops were finally delivering an ultimatum, we pulled ourselves together, and peeled back the curtain to find Anna standing there with breakfast. Boy was she a sight for sore eyes and an empty stomach. That day we were treated to the best of Vienna as Anna shouted our entry to the city museums and galleries. That night she took us to her mum's for a home-cooked meal. It was a huge feast with enough schnitzel and potato carbs to keep us going for days. We couldn't thank Anna and mum enough.

Feeling a lot more positive we went to the post office the next day and asked if the transfer had come through. The people there knew us by now and were smiling this time. Unfortunately, the money could only be paid in Austrian currency, which we then changed into an assortment of other currencies, losing each time on the hefty exchange fees. With a pocket full of cash and new traveller's cheques we were ready to hit the road. It was time to head south to Yugoslavia.

We were fortunate to travel through Yugoslavia (Croatia) before the ethnic wars of the nineties. It was a socialist state at the time, comprised of a number of small republics which were formed after the German occupation of World War Two. President Tito was in control and every building displayed his picture. We planned to travel along the mountain range that ran through the centre of the country, down to Zagreb first and then to Sarajevo before heading west for the coast and Split.

It was still very cold in the mountains and there was lots of snow about. The living conditions were very spartan and in places we got our first taste of a male-dominated Muslim society. Not a lot of women around and those that were all wore head scarfs. On this first leg our van got stuck in the snow a few times so we couldn't clutch start it. The locals were helpful but the one time the police offered assistance they wanted to be paid. They weren't impressed when we didn't cough up but luckily we were building up speed and didn't look back. In one town Pedro went to buy some food and came back with five kilos of dried figs. He said it was the only food in the market. One couldn't complain about the price, but the van got pretty smelly after a few days of eating them.

Down at Split it was a completely different scene, abundant markets and rich in ancient maritime and Christian history. Here we visited some friends of my parents who cooked up a big meal and topped it off with the local peach schnapps. It was firewater! Thankfully we only had a short "walk" to the van where we passed out. After about two hours we awoke, wet with sweat and with an amazing sense of clarity. The late night card game was fun as I'm sure we could read each other's hidden cards.

The next morning we sat with the van door open drinking tea and looking out over the medieval fort and port. It was such a beautiful place and we were so glad to be amongst it. It was such a big change from our life back home where the only contemplation was which party should we go to next. Seeing this history and culture was really grounding and made us appreciate what had gone before us and our place in the world.

Early that afternoon we headed up the coast towards Venice. What a dangerous road! Just a skinny ribbon running around the high cliffs, complete with landslips and burnt-out mangled cars and trucks at the bottom of ravines. How we got through it I'll never know. It was like navigating through a video game landscape. It got even more surreal with petrochemical industrialisation as we got closer to Italy.

Endless factories belching out crap. It was scary, horrible and filthy. And then it was replaced by the beauty and calm of Venice, the seaport trading heart of the world for centuries. We managed to park in a nice quiet area on the mainland and bussed it into the town. It was amazing walking around the cobble stone streets, bridges and waterways and listening to the gondoliers singing. The city was rich in art and beautifully kept, but very expensive, and a few too many tourists to relax. I'm pretty sure we came back for a second day to see the eleventh century St Mark's Basilica and the gothic Doge's Palace which was built in the thirteen hundreds as the residence for the head of the Venetian republic. It was a short but artistically stimulating visit.

We then drove down the entire east coast of Italy, through all the coastal towns and ancient fortifications. It was the off-season, all the beach resorts were closed and it was easy to get around. The water was still warm so we had a dip whenever we could. We felt very much at home with the large number of eucalyptus trees and oleander bushes that lined the roadways. We couldn't work out if the trees grew naturally in Italy or were brought back from Australia and planted there to reminisce.

The food in Italy was great and it was cheap, but we mostly bought or roadside-picked the ingredients and cooked for ourselves. At lunchtimes we would make a point of buying bread, cheese, salami, and wine, and eating at some pretty country or beach-side stop.

Once we got down to Bari we headed west through Calabria to Villa San Giovanni where we put the van on a ferry to Messina in Sicily. Amazingly we managed to find and park the van in a long-term storage garage so we could get a boat out to the islands where my oldies had come from. The garage attendant directed us to a spot right next to Octopus' Bedford panel van. So funny. We had seen it in London and thought their fifty quid purchase would never make it outside England. They had obviously headed off to the islands ahead of us.

That afternoon we took the hydrofoil ferry north to the Aeolian islands. The shuttle included dockings at Vulcano, Lipari,

Salina and then our stop on Panarea, where we stayed with my dad's Aunty Rosalina for about a week. It was pretty spartan living but the view out over the Med was amazing. We couldn't speak Italian and Rosalina couldn't speak English. She made sensational, simple meals and somehow we conversed.

Back in the nineteen twenties my grandmother was the town butcher. The family owned about fifteen small parcels of land. All were acquired by my grandfather who returned every year from his merchant navy duties to buy land and leave another baby. The women were the strong ones. They had to etch out a living from the goats, chickens and vegetables while raising a herd of children. Unfortunately, over subsequent years all the land was stolen or sold off and someone else benefited from the jet-set super yachts and rich tourists that now holiday the island.

One day we decided to circumnavigate the island but we quickly ran out of beach track and had to start swimming. We figured the next beach was just around the headland but the cliff faces just got longer and it ended up being a three kilometre swim … a slow breast-stroke. Along the way I saw a real octopus gliding through the water so I dived down and grabbed him, turned him inside out and put him in my trunks. We finally got to a beach where, thankfully, it was just a short walk back to the house. There, I proudly presented my catch to the old Aunty who was amazed, and she cooked him up that night in the pasta sauce.

The next day we took a small ferry to the island of Stromboli which was about two to three kilometres away. Stromboli was basically a pyramid-shaped volcano island. It was smoking which the locals said was good because it was releasing the pressure. Down one face there was a stream of molten rocks rolling and steaming into the sea.

There is a saying that Stromboli men are all bald because of the falling ash. One of my uncles had come from this island and he was bald. We went to check out his old house. It turned out to be a small stone cottage that had been rendered and painted white. The current owners had painted the timber windows and doors a nice shade of lime green. Very cute next to the ones that had orange and the ones that had blue trim. Every house had a small garden growing the essentials. At the end of his street was a path leading up the hill so we decided to go someway up the volcano. As we climbed the view out over the water and the other distant islands was amazing.

We were being lured to the top so we kept climbing. It was a long, slow march through the rich black-coked soil and it was really, really hot. Thankfully, every time we turned around the view over the Med just got better and better and we were cooled with the sea breeze. As we got close to the top the noise of the occasional bursts of lava spewing out started to get very un-nerving. We eventually and tentatively climbed to the quieter side of the rim and looked in. After the quick photo we turned around and quickly headed down. It was just too scary. We knew the chances of it really going off were slim but there was always the chance of a small puff of lava heading our way. We weren't prepared to push our luck any further.

Back on Panarea we found where my cousins had been staying but we had missed them by a day. They had gone to the island of Lipari. Unfortunately, our time had come to an end in this paradise so we said goodbye to Rosalina and our new friends and boarded the ferry back to Messina.

Despite some of the rumours about thieves our van was still there, but Occy's van was gone, so counting our lucky stars and trying to make sense of the roads we headed out. We made it up into the mountains at the back of Palermo to Corleone which was made famous by *The Godfather*. Then we went to a small village named Porgaregale which was Occy's parent's hometown. It had been destroyed by an earthquake earlier so there wasn't much to see but there on the side of the road in a small cul-de-sac was the Bedford van. It was an Italian hugging reunion with a ceremonial cup of English Breakfast tea.

My cousins were in a state of shock as they had been kidnapped in Palermo for four hours. Apparently, Nell had been walking alone when some boys dragged her into a van and demanded money. About fifteen minutes later Octopus passed by looking for her, so they grabbed him as well. When they eventually realised there was no money the boys threw them out and called them everything under the sun. Octopus tried to engage the first policeman he saw, but all he got was a shrug of the shoulders.

Occy and Nell were also very excited to tell us they were expecting a baby and heading back to Australia the next day by plane. They were going to abandon their car. I jokingly said: "I'll have the starter motor". It bolted straight in and worked first time. A true advertisement for the development that went into English automotive parts over a thirty year period, and $500 saved.

Travelling the next leg of the trip was a luxury. No more clutch starts. It was strange having Pedro there by my side as we drove off.

We thought we'd get seriously adventurous and bought tickets for the ferry from Palermo to Tunisia in North Africa. The idea was to drive across Tunisia into Algeria and then Morocco and then back into Spain. It was a late-night boarding that fortunately, or unfortunately, didn't happen. The Australian Government had only just changed the arrangement it had with Tunisia and you now needed a visa which could only be issued in Rome. We were really disappointed as we'd been dreaming about this part of the trip for weeks, but we got a refund and headed back to the mainland.

Back in Italy we wanted to save the tolls on the Autostrada north, so we stuck to the goat track coastal roads. It was slow going but turned out to be a blessing. We passed through the beautiful towns of Salerno, Ravello, Positano, Sorrento and on to Naples, where we spent a day in Pompeii and climbed Mount Vesuvius, another volcano. Vesuvius was dormant, but as we could see from the destruction in Pompeii it was capable of devastating activity. Naples, or the city of thieves as it was known then, is an amazing city built on the side of that volcano. You kind of wonder how relaxing it would be living in a city that could be blown apart again one day. Even with warning there would be no way of getting out, as the roads were jammed at the best of times.

We then drove up to Rome and stayed outside the university where we unloaded the pushies and explored the history of the place. We got to the Vatican and some other "must sees" but we tried to conserve our entrance fee money. There were plenty of alternatives as there was something to see on every corner. Rome is one of the great cities of the world. And the girls are the most beautiful. I wish my Italian had been better.

After a week we moved on. This time carrying two American students who we had picked up from a share-petrol ride sign we posted at the uni. I don't know what we were thinking. They turned out to be such a pain that we kicked them out somewhere between Pisa and Genoa. Literally pulled over on the side of the road, threw their backpacks out, and when they went to get them, drove off. What a relief! They whined like a fucked diff from the moment we set out. It was so much more relaxed without them as we burbled around the Italian Riviera to Monaco, Nice, Cannes and the eternal seaport city of Marseilles, before heading north to Paris. On the way up to Paris we passed through a lot of farmland and more than once stopped to ask the farmers if we could work as pickers. The result was always a "non" so we would drive on a bit further and do some unpaid picking, "oui".

As we approached Paris we kept seeing girls with next to nothing on standing by roadside fires. It was very strange but we soon realised they were waiting for drive-bys. It turned out they were mostly Eastern European "gypsy" women who had made their way to France illegally. We were sad for them having to stand around half naked in the freezing cold, in the middle of nowhere, and selling their bodies so their pimps could take most of their earnings. We ended up camping in the woods nearby and making daily bus trips into the city centre. The things that went on in those woods around campfires were grotesque so there wasn't a lot of sleeping. We kept thinking of the Stones song *Too Much Blood* where the Japanese guy ate his date and buried her bones in the Bois de Boulogne (our campground). Paris was so beautiful and really helped offset our less-than-perfect lodgings.

Back in London we remembered an invite from the girls on the boat and headed to North Finchley where we met expat stockbroker Paul Mac. He was the boyfriend of one of the girls and was keen to rent us the last remaining room in a terrace house he had just bought. Pedro and I shared the room. There were five of us living in Paul's three bedroom and one bathroom house. It was a great little community. We took it in turns cooking and we learnt a lot about football. It was on every TV channel all the time.

It was getting close to Christmas so we had a look around for some work. It was pretty hard going so we ended up joining an agency and secured jobs with a Swiss Bank. It was one strange experience. We turned up for the first day of work at a disused bank building in the centre of London. We were shown to an office on the second floor. We were the only ones in the building. A Scotsman entered the room and welcomed us and explained that he wanted us to check computer readouts. In one of the rooms there were mountains of these continuous dot-matrix printouts of financial information.

The Scotsman wasn't the easiest guy to understand. He had the thickest accent. We actually couldn't understand a word he was saying. We nodded at the end of his rave and asked him to recap the role. He had another go, and at the end of it, not wanting to appear like total idiots we said "okay". He left the building and we looked at one another and laughed. We then looked at the computer printouts and really couldn't work out what he wanted us to do with them. We then checked out the rest of the building. It was empty. We were the only ones there. They had another building next door and it was where the rest of the staff had their offices.

I said it was strange but it turned out to be a blessing. During the four weeks we were there no one came back to check on us. No one. We just turned up every day to Bundy on so we got paid. We brought Pedro's world map with us and pinned it up on the wall and started planning the overland leg of our trip. We then split resources. One stayed in the office to provide cover in case someone turned up. The other took the passports and visa applications off to the Turkey, Iran, Afghanistan, Pakistan and Indian embassies.

We enrolled in an Anthropology course at the university to get our Student ID Cards and tried to find out as much as possible about the trip. After a week we came to the realisation that there was no formal information. The best we got, and it was pretty flimsy, was from a university notice board. Someone else's experiences and advice. Who would have known that in the future most people would treat other people's reviews as gospel and the only way to travel? Wished we had got on to that one earlier.

We still had a little bit of money left over from our Europe trip and we thought about driving our van overland. In the end it was going to be a lot more than we could afford. As it turned out driving a vehicle overland was nothing but drama. For a start it was winter and there was snow and ice. And the people who we did meet on our trip spent days at borders getting in and out. They were constantly harassed by kids and thieves. The repairs were very dodgy and spare parts were non-existent. The roads were very dangerous and the maps were unreliable. Some vans were covered in steel mesh to keep the things and their occupants secure from theft and attack.

With no further European driving planned we sold the van. It took about two hours and we got our money back. Funnily when we emptied the van we found two rogue teabags at the back of the cupboard, which we immediately brewed as a thank you salute to Queenie.

During our time in "Swinging London" we went to a few concerts – saw Jethro Tull and some reggae acts. The music scene in London was different to the pub rock scene in Sydney. The acts and venues were bigger and the tickets were harder to get. We managed to go to a couple of Speedway race nights at White City Stadium. Speedway was really big in Europe and we cheered on the Aussie world cup riders Crump, Boulger, Sanders and Herne. We also frequented the local pub where we sat on a pint for most of the night, learned to play darts and pool, and made loads of new friends.

There were lots of Aussies in London. Most at Earl's Court or, as the Poms (the English) called it, Kangaroo Valley. There was nowhere in Australia like it … a large concentration of young people exchanging ideas in a global community. London was a really stimulating destination and the fashion was really out there and Carnaby Street was the place to see it. If you could afford to buy a piece from there you were definitely in the groove.

Other memorable London activities included the Turner Exhibition, and a Beatles pilgrimage to Abbey Road and the Apple Records studio on Savile Row.

As we were getting close to departing we decided to buy a $70, thirty-day Eurail Pass so we could catch up on a few places we had missed when vanning around. The idea was to slowly make our way across to Athens - the last European city before hitting the great junction between east and west in Istanbul. It was a sad day donning backpacks and saying farewells to our "English family" but very exciting as we headed to the local train station and on to Victoria Station and the train to Brussels.

We arrived in Brussels fairly late so wandered around checking out the red light district and the girls sitting in the windows displaying their wares. We didn't know where to go to find a budget hotel so we looked for a place to sleep and settled on a department store doorway off the street. It was a pretty miserable night. It was freezing, the ground was marble hard and cold as ice. No one hassled us, thank God. The next morning we found a café with coffee and a pastry, and after the cold left our bones all was right with the world.

One night down. We had managed to avoid paying for accommodation, so that became the ongoing challenge. We decided to sight-see during the day and take our trains at night. No sleeper carriages, just sit-up seats. Some trains had big luggage racks where you could climb up, stretch out and get some sleep. I remember waking one night to see the police checking passports below as I quietly looked on and waited for them to leave. At one point I thought I should speak up but the longer I left it the more difficult it became, so I pretended to be asleep until they left.

From Brussels we headed to Paris and from there we trained it through France and into the night. The next morning we changed trains and headed to Biarritz to check out the only known European surf break at the time. Funny it had some surf shops similar to those on Sydney's beaches, but instead of golden sands this was a break-wall village with cobble stone streets. The surf looked cold, grey and choppy. There was no way I was going in.

We then made our way down to San Sebastian on the north coast of Spain and on to Barcelona. Whilst there we climbed through Gaudi's cathedral. Then it was a YMCA bed for the night before taking the train to Lisbon in Portugal.

After a quick look around Lisbon and sampling as many of their fish dishes as we could, we got back on a south-bound train to Gibraltar, and then took a ferry across to Tangiers in Morocco.

The tone of the trip changed in Morocco. It was chaos. Almost immediately young touts picked us up and were recommending cheap hotels. They appeared friendly until we wouldn't let them come into our room. They got really aggro so Pedro shunted them away from the door, and then out came the knives. We quickly slammed the door. They started swearing and spitting at us through the transom window over the doorway. They eventually buggered off but they did leave us quite shaken and it took a while before we ventured back out into the street. We knew we weren't in the safety of Europe anymore so we got our smarts on.

The next day we checked out the Medina market where I bought a pair of goatskin jeans. They looked really cool but they must have still been tanning them as they stank my backpack out for months. Despite the smell they turned out to be a saviour in the cold of Turkey and Afghanistan.

After exploring all we could we headed for the bus station - it was set around a giant square - and eventually found a local bus heading for Casablanca. It was a long trip and we stopped along the way a few times for sugar-loaded mint tea and toilet breaks. These toilet stops were an introduction to rudimentary relief and got worse the further we went south.

Casablanca was a bustling hub that possessed some fantastic French colonial architecture. Many buildings were fortress-like on the outside which secured a garden courtyard often built around a giant tree. Such a nice vibe. It was an overcast day so we headed for the beach where we sipped mint tea and watched the waves crash in and the camel trains pass by.

We then bussed it on to Marrakesh with Crosby, Stills and Nash playing in our heads. We experienced a local market and tasted the local foods. There were some great walks up through the hills but mostly we stayed close to the town for safety.

Over the next few days we travelled by bus through the Atlas Mountains to Fez where we spent a couple of nights. Here we explored the endless market alleys and got lost in Arab medieval time. We bought some fine cut grass called kif and a long pipe to smoke it, and whilst contemplating the rugged mountain landscape we read *Smokestack El Ropo's Bedside Reader*, a compendium of marijuana-related stories from Morocco written by Rolling Stone magazine journalist, Charles Perry.

After arriving back in Tangiers we realised we had probably spent a few too many days in Morocco as we had a little over twenty four hours left on our Eurail Pass. To fully utilise the pass we needed to get a ferry back to Gibraltar and trains all the way around to Brindisi on the south east coast of Italy. That was a big trip and there was no way it was going to happen in the time but we wanted to roll the dice anyway.

Luckily there was a ferry just about to leave and the passage across the Straits of Gibraltar was fairly smooth. We then boarded a waiting train that would take us all the way up through Spain and on to Marseilles, where we immediately connected with a train to get us to Genoa and then another to Rome and, in the middle of the night, yet another that got us to Brindisi at about six am. We made it! Double sixes! It was crazy how it just worked. Thankfully there were no "ritardo" rail connections along the way. We'd heard horror stories about the Italian rail system but we had proved it wrong!

The Brindisi city map at the railway station gave us all the info we needed. We wandered around the old port town, had an early morning coffee and pastry and at nine o'clock made our way to the ferry. We had just enough time to use our Eurail pass one last time to get a half price ferry ticket to Greece. Talk about value!

The ship was an older-style cargo and passenger boat which we boarded via gang plank and made our way to the upper deck, where there was a small group of travellers. Two guys and a girl that looked like they were in their twenties. As it turned out they were Americans who had the same overland trip in mind.

Pedro and I introduced ourselves to Olga, Troy and Ryan. The three had met in the Canary Islands, a Spanish archipelago off the north-west African coast. The stories from the islands were amazing. They had spent three months there and it sounded like an idyllic hippie scene with full moon acid parties and naked beach bathing a norm.

Olga was a couple of years older than us and from New York. She was a beautiful girl, loud and engaging with big eyes and expressive hands. She had wild long brown hair, a T-shirt, no bra, rolled up overalls and thongs. She could be a New Yorker when she wanted but couldn't contain her Puerto Rican background. Either way she was loud and the centre of the party. Her kit was a knitted overnight bag that made our backpacks look like sea trunks.

We raved and laughed as the ship headed out. I think Pedro and I were the first Aussies they had come across as the Canary Islands were full of French, Spanish and English. They couldn't believe our accents. When they heard we were heading overland to India, and that we had a bigger clue than they did about what might lie ahead, they suggested we travel some way together.

As it turned out Troy was about thirty-five and had grown up on the west coast of the States. He had an old surfer vibe, shaggy collar-length hair, clean shaven and amber lensed glasses. He wore old embroidered jeans, a white T-shirt and lent on his leather duffle bag. He was quick to let us know he was gay … but he didn't mince about. He was the first gay guy I had met … well one that was open about it anyway. He was well educated and I think he worked in education. Troy loved to smoke hash. While living in the Canary Islands he'd collected an array of implements and devices to enhance the smoking experience whilst delivering the best possible stone. He reminisced about leaving them behind. Troy was to never let a smoking opportunity go by. He grabbed each with a twinkle in his eye and as though it was going to be his last.

GET YOUR MOTOR RUNNING

Ryan was twenty-two and from the mid-west of the U.S. He was recently out of college and looked it. His hair was growing out, he had a moustache and his polo, chinos and Sperrys were just getting worn in. He was having a good time. I think his oldies had money so he didn't have any restrictions. As it turned out Ryan liked to keep up with Troy in the smoking department. He also liked acid and could sniff out fellow trippers no matter where and who they were. He would often disappear and come back holding enough to get us all high. I loved the way acid heads helped each other out.

It was day one of the big adventure. Our little group had grown. There was now a crazy chick, a smoking fiend and an acid head. It was starting to get interesting.

We disembarked in Port Piraeus intending to head into Athens but were seduced by the ferries heading to the beautiful Greek Islands. Mykonos looked fantastic so with an easy "yes" vote we all bought tickets. It was early afternoon when we arrived and the island was just so beautiful in the sun. With directions from the locals we set out from the wharf and headed to a hotel. When we arrived we took three rooms. Olga suggested she share one with me. Pedro took a room with Ryan and Troy went solo. I couldn't believe my luck I was going to share with the crazy chick.

I was hoping that we would share more than the room and Olga had the same idea. No sooner had we dropped our bags than she was getting her gear off to shower. She was a package, all over tan, nice breasts, good hips, full bottom, and a bushy hippie crutch and underarms. We couldn't help getting straight into it. She really enjoyed getting it on and was unlike any girl I'd been with before. We had a great couple of days in Mykonos.

Olga was really smart, very political, a Capricorn and a John Lennon *Imagine* recruit. She believed that religion and politics were screwing things up and was into the brotherhood of man. It endeared her to a lot of people and later on it was to prove a great asset in some pretty hectic situations. She wore a long necklace made from the smooth brown seeds of the sacred Bodhi Gaya fig-tree under which Buddha attained enlightenment. The tree grows near Patna in India and is a direct descendent of the original tree of 288 BC. There are two other descendants of the tree - Ananada Bodhi growing near Lucknow in India, and Bodhi Anuradhapura which grows in the central north of Sri Lanka. A meditation/yoga friend had given her these beads in New York. They were her treasure.

I remember sitting down to a late lunch on the first day and within minutes Ryan had scored some acid from another American in the restaurant. That night all five of us took the acid and sat on the large concrete retainer blocks at the harbour while a huge storm pounded us with giant waves and the blocks vibrated. We held each other tight so as not to be swept away and really got into each other's minds as we all became one with the storm.

There was lots of sunbathing and sea dips on Mykonos and the evening meals were so much fun. We ate in a large restaurant with twenty to thirty others and after the meal, out came the Ouzo shots (a fennel or anise-flavoured liquor) and then the dancing … and the plates. I'd never seen it before. They had piles of small plates and started throwing them on the floor. We threw our share and danced amongst the broken crockery. It was very funny and got wilder by the shot glass. The headaches the next day were pretty intense, so after a few nights of this we needed to get the ferry back to Athens.

On the boat Olga was fiddling around in her bag and pulled out her tarot cards. She was very skilled having been taught by gypsy women in Puerto Rico and New York. The cards read well so all was good in love and travel. During this ferry ride I learned a lot more about Olga. She was an Arts graduate and had worked as an escort while trying to make ends meet in New York. She was a part of the hippie scene and one of the first to go up to Woodstock when the festival was announced. There was a big arts community living up in the area and she bunked in and helped the locals pull the infrastructure together. Olga saw all the festival acts and thought Sly and the Family Stone and Jimi were the standouts. I was in awe after that. She had actually seen Jimi play, and more than once, as she had also seen him at the New York Pop Festival. It was like being in the presence of one of the Apostles.

Athens was a beautiful city. Very run down and in need of a good clean, but nevertheless a town steeped in ancient history. We arrived at a small hotel which, after a bit of negotiation, ended up the right price. It was here Olga and I met an early twenties, German guy called Little, who looked like he'd come straight out of the mountains of Tibet. He called me Baba which was a quirky Persian/Indian name given to a friend, father or expert.

Little was wearing a long Indian cotton shirt and balloon pants, an embroidered waistcoat, sandals, multiple beads and bangles, and a huge multi-coloured embroidered hat with three upturned yak-fur flaps. He was very friendly and when he heard we were heading overland he invited us back to his room to talk some more. Once in there he opened his waistcoat and smiled. It was full of pockets with a variety of chillum pipes tucked into each. They were fired clay cylinders, each about six inches in length, funnelling down to a small opening at the bottom. A small stone was loosely lodged at the base to hold the mull.

He then unrolled a silk tummy wrap to proudly show off a kilo of the best black Afghani hash one could imagine. I'd never seen a kilo before. It was a flat brick about ten inches by five inches and a quarter of an inch thick. When the plastic came off, it had a gold zero-zero stamp to show its quality and smelt like sweet pollen. Little said that it was the number one primo gear.

After telling us he paid about fifty dollars for the brick and explaining how one went about buying hash in quantity, he carefully wrapped and strapped it back on his person. He then pulled a small block of about ten grams from one of his many pockets and heated one side so it crumbled off in his fingers. He then broke a cigarette down and mixed the hash into the tobacco which he then stuffed into his prized chillum. It was his Shiva pipe. Decorated with images of the Indian ganga-smoking deity Shiva. As I watched him working, it reminded me of a priest preparing the challis for a spiritual offering. He was a Chillum Baba!

In reverend style he pulled out a small gauze cloth, dampened it in water and wrapped it around the bottom end of the pipe to cool the clay and catch any rogue embers. He held it between his clasped hands, called out "Bom! Bom!" and put the bottom end to his lips as Olga put a match to it. My God! I couldn't believe how he sucked that thing into life and the extraordinary amount of smoke he blew out. His room was really small and I don't think it even had a window. Within seconds the room was a blanket of smoke. He passed the flaming pipe on to Olga who chugged away on it and then it was my turn. I approached it cautiously and was surprised at how easily the cool smoke filled my lungs. There was coughing and spluttering as the pipe went around the circle a few times. I could hardly see the others for the smoke and it started to freak me that the hotel staff would call the cops.

I was whacked and couldn't really go anywhere, so as the stone settled in I watched Little clean the pipe with a small hemp rope pull-through. He then wrapped it in the cool gauze and put it back in its pocket.

In the hour or so we were with him he told us that he was returning to Germany after running away from compulsory national service. He intended turning up at his homeland border crossing like he had done in India, Pakistan, Afghanistan, Iran, Turkey and Greece. How he got that far, dressed like that, I will never know. I could only imagine the reception he was in for if he made it back to Germany, especially as a wanted man and with that brick of hash. Little was a beautiful soul. I truly wished him a lot of luck.

After that little episode we were intrigued at what might lay ahead of us and knew we were on the edge of one giant adventure. But there were still a few things to do. We had planned to take the train to Istanbul and move quickly on to Tehran, as winter was settling in and we just wanted to get to the sunshine on the other side as quickly as possible. We had been pretty frugal with our money up to this point and we knew that our time away was directly proportionate to the money we had on us. We had heard horror stories about getting money wired to banks along the way and figured our experience in Austria was nothing compared to what could happen, so we had to make sure our cash and travellers cheques lasted till we could get back to a reasonably urbane city. And we had to be super careful about not getting ripped off.

The word on the street was that the hospital was paying people to donate blood. So, with the chance of adding a few dollars to the kitty we went off to investigate. It was all legit. It was the first time I had given blood so it was kind of scary. Looking back I'm not sure the hygiene was up to the standards in Australia but it did mean we found out our blood types which we recorded on our Health Cards and we had some unexpected money to pay for our train ticket and the next leg of the journey.

Your health card was a mini passport and had the same importance. You needed to show evidence that you were immunised for cholera, smallpox and malaria to get across the borders. Luckily, we had all this done in Sydney before we left. Our poor arms after those shots. They went dead and were tender and itchy for about a week. One had to really resist scratching the needled area to prevent permanent scarring. I could only imagine how terrible it would be to catch the full-blown disease. Keeping the shots up to date turned out to be a bit of a nightmare as it meant having to go to dodgy clinics along the way and have them inject shitty serums into you. We were very careful and often hung out to get to a clean, reputable surgery before allowing any bodily intervention.

With blood money in hand we bought tickets on a train scheduled to leave in two days time. To conserve money we ate cheap souvlaki take-aways for what seemed like breakfast, lunch and dinner as we explored the archaeology and tried to understand what was really a Greek tragedy. The poor old Greeks weren't preserving their treasures. I'd done Ancient History as a subject at school and was quite interested in Greek and Roman civilisation. I was appalled at the state of the ruins and museums. There was absolutely no maintenance and not a lot of relics. I remembered the awesome collections in the museums of the Vatican, Paris and London and realised how later civilisations had plundered and pillaged the best of everything. On reflection it was probably a good thing as they would surely have been broken, stolen, recycled or destroyed by idiots.

Our good friend Ryan had been busy and came back with trips that we unleashed on the Parthenon that night. There was no one around so we set up in the Amphitheatre, role-played some classics and called on the Greek gods. The night passed quickly and it was dawn before we came back down into the city to hunt out an early breakfast. Strangely the streets were crowded and people were banging each other with toy hammers to celebrate some festival. It was too bizarre for us so we retreated to the hotel and slept for the rest of the day.

It was time to leave. I remember boarding the train with Olga, Pedro, Troy and Ryan and looking around one last time and thinking how we were leaving the world as we knew it and heading into the great unknown. I wasn't scared as I had our little collective around me but it was definitely a turning point in my life and I knew that I had to be super strong to come out the other end. It was great knowing that Pedro had my back and that Olga was a comforting friend.

The train turned out to be driven by a steam engine and after a lot of commotion it gathered speed and wound its way out of Greece leaving a rail of smoke as it entered the evening darkness. The hillside villages soon passed and as the night went on the imprint of humanity got denser and denser as we headed to the Bosphorus and ancient Constantinople, modern day Istanbul.

CHAPTER FOUR

Dweller On The Threshold

The next morning we arrived at Istanbul's main station. It was hectic. Thankfully some kids picked us up and we walked to a large budget-style hotel. After check-in we set out to explore the city. It was amazing. The religious capital of the world for a thousand years. So vibrant and yet so old. You could easily imagine you were a medieval trader as you moved around the port, the fishing boats and through the oldest covered market in the world, the Grand Bazaar. We made a special point of crossing the Bosphorus bridge and stepping onto Asian soil for the first time. In a few short days we would leave the civilisation of Europe and enter another world. Looking back, I felt like Van Morrison's *Dweller on the Threshold* and was waiting at the door.

The tea shops of Istanbul were a refuge and hosted a flow of travellers of all races and religions. Some in a hurry, and some just killing time sipping, reading and smoking. The more traditional ones offered a shisha package of flavoured tobacco, a hot coal and a hubble bubble water pipe. And if lucky they'd throw a small nick of hash on top. Their notice boards were full of messages, dozens of them, some person-to-person chats, a lot of private and commercial buses looking for passengers, as well as business cards for hotels, taxis and hot baths … and in multiple languages.

DWELLER ON THE THRESHOLD

This was the first time I felt the camaraderie of travellers. The tourists were gone. We had left them in Athens. This was a new breed moving from the first world to the outposts of another land … and there were awakened people heading back the other way.

The Pudding Shop or the Lale Restaurant was the place to hang out. It was a bohemian rhapsody that had been going since the sixties and was still strong. The restaurant was nothing special but the owners offered western food and music. It was also a transport pick up point. There were lots of old, clapped-out vans and buses coming through from Amsterdam, London, Paris and Munich. All heading for India or places in between. Many were just "heads" looking for people to share a joint and the cost of petrol. Some of the buses operated just to cover the cost of their owners staying on the road. Some were commercial enterprises, and some were covering for it. For years they travelled back and forward and often came home a little heavier with hidden kilos of hashish to be sold and the money used to upgrade their wheels and supplement their next journey.

These drivers were strange people, hardened with the challenges and dangers of the road, but optimistic and flexible. There were no deadlines to meet. If the bus broke down or the passengers got sick they would just wait until everyone was ready for the next leg. Some of the more professional bus companies tried to keep to a timetable as they had passengers waiting at the other end to get home but they, like everyone else, were at the mercy of the road.

We spied some great fares, $22 from Istanbul to Delhi, but we didn't want to be constrained by someone else's agenda. We were going to make our own way … and in our own time.

Istanbul opened our eyes to new foods and their preparation. Some tasty treats especially the sweets. Some shockers when it came to the meats. The butcher shops were just that. A place where butchering went on and hygiene was gone. It was at this point that we added no meat to the no ciggies and no drink. It was going to be vego cuisine from here on out.

That night Pedro and Ryan headed out a Turkish steam bath, while Olga and I stayed behind and went to the shower room on our floor. We locked ourselves in and tried to light the gas hot water heater. The instructions were in multiple languages but we just couldn't get it to light, and we couldn't turn it off either. The room was filling fast with gas. We tried to open the door to get out, but it was jammed. How could this be happening? We started to panic. It felt like we were in one of those movies. We got down low and launched our shoulders into the door hoping we could budge it. Within seconds two Pakistani guys came barging in, they knocked us onto our arses and the door broke off its hinges. Then with a twist of this lever and that, they turned the gas off. It was such a relief. Really weird, we couldn't believe it and were very, very thankful. They nodded their heads sideways as if to say 'it was nothing", and invited us to have drinks in their room. What could we say? They had saved our lives.

Their room was huge … a suite … and there were about ten guys in there. Apprehensively we entered and were introduced to Abdul, who was obviously the head guy, as he was sitting at a big desk handing out the orders. He had a carton of Benson and Hedges Gold and a bottle of Johnny Walker Black on display. They were on their way home to Pakistan after doing business in Germany. Abdul asked if we wanted to have a drink and poured the scotch. We thought it a little weird that he was drinking alcohol as we didn't think muslims were allowed, but although Abdul wore traditional garb, he was very western looking. He toasted our health and we thanked his men once more. Abdul then asked if we wanted to smoke hash. Olga was quick to reply.

We knew we couldn't do it in the room as the police were heavy around the hotels, so we went out into the street. Pedro and Ryan arrived back and when they found out where we were heading Pedro said he was keen to come along. Abdul agreed. Ryan left us, and soon after an old Mercedes saloon pulled up. We got in the back with Abdul, and there were two others in front with the driver. We drove out of Istanbul and into the countryside. It took forever and it felt like we had driven to Albania. Then we stopped in the middle of nowhere. It was now dark. There were no lights or houses. We started to get a bit freaked. What were we doing there in the back of the car with all these guys? I was worried for Olga and quietly fiddled around in my pocket for my penknife. It was there but I couldn't open the blade.

We waited nervously in the dark, making small talk for what seemed like fifteen minutes. Then lights appeared in the distance ahead of us. Flashing from a car. Our car flashed back. Two of our guys got out and walked off into the darkness.

About ten minutes and an eternity later they came back, alone, thank god, and handed a small packet of hashish in through the window to the driver and he passed it back to Abdul. Abdul then emptied a cigarette by rolling it between his fingers until the tobacco became a powder and fell out the end. He then heated the corner of the hash with a match and crumbled it into the fine tobacco, and then refilled the cigarette. After all that we finally got to smoke.

Abdul held the ciggie between his index fingers and made a clasped fist with both hands - all he needed to do was suck through his widened thumbs. Good hygiene. He passed it around and we smoked it the same way. We got very stoned and as there wasn't a lot to talk about we asked to go back to the hotel. They weren't too keen and put the radio on and started singing and swaying their arms. We were miles from anywhere and far from being in any sort of control. Somehow after lots of giggling and laughing on their part we were returned safely to our hotel.

We got to know the 'Pakis' a bit over the next few days. They were good people. There were about twelve of them and they had a small fleet of secondhand Mercedes cars that they were ferrying into Pakistan to be used as taxis. There was a ringleader, his lieutenants and the worker bees. I'm sure their scam was to create confusion so they could get the vehicles through the border crossings without paying duty. One guy had all the passports, one guy had the vehicle carnets, one had the registrations, one had the health cards, one had the keys and one had the cash just in case. All of them shouting at the one time. The poor customs guys would have been glad to see the back of them and no doubt could only shrug their shoulders when a number of the cars made it through without documentation.

One of the most impressive sights in Istanbul was the Hagia Sophia. It was the largest dome building on earth when constructed by Roman Emperor Constantius in 537AD and became the Christian Cathedral of the world. It was damaged and rebuilt a number of times during almost one thousand years of Roman occupation, and in the 1450s the city fell to the Ottoman siege led by Sultan Mehmed and the Hagia Sophia then became the Imperial Mosque. The mosaic floors and ceilings are a true marvel and engender a deep respect for previous civilisations.

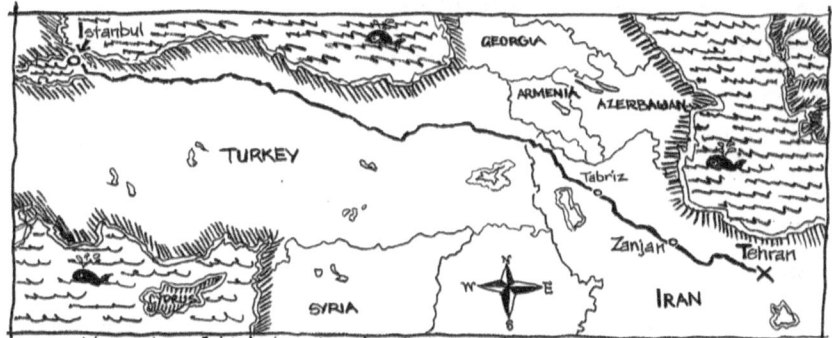

It was time to leave Istanbul, we boarded the trail to Tehran, 2,500 kms — 3 days man!!

It was time to move on. With backpacks, and in trepidation, we boarded the train for Tehran. Luckily we got into a carriage with a compartment seating six, we closed the door and made ourselves comfortable. It was going to be a two thousand five hundred kilometre, three-day trip so we settled into our books.

As we headed east the landscape changed and it got colder. Outside was a snow-covered barren desert landscape. It looked like what I imagined Siberia to be. I was so glad to be on the train and not on one of those buses, on the road, out in the elements.

After a day of rattling along, the Iranian immigration police arrived for a visa pre-inspection. They looked at Pedro and my passports and started chatting amongst themselves. Then one who was good at English said there was an issue and took the passports away. We had no idea what it was about. About four hours later they returned and asked us to follow them to a carriage at the back of the train. There we were interviewed for about an hour and then allowed to return to our carriage, but without our passports.

The train stopped late that night. It was a tiny station with a one-room shed on the platform. The police said we needed to leave the train. We looked outside at the snow and desolate surrounds and said "no way". It was a stand-off. Pedro puffed up his chest and stood tall and in his big voice demanded to go to the Embassy in Tehran. I stepped up and stood next to him. The police were in shock, and not accustomed to being challenged rethought their position. We were allowed to stay on board the train. The relief we felt was amazing when that train moved off. Imagine being stuck out in the middle of nowhere in that snow. They had to be joking!

We were then ushered back to the police carriage where they interrogated us one at a time. It was finally revealed there was a problem with the visa stamp that we got in London. The date that had been hand-written on the visa stamp had been changed. We had no idea as it was written in Persian. Obviously the embassy staff had made a mistake and written over it. We denied knowing anything about it.

The police suggested that we spend a few nights at the police station in Tehran while they contacted their Embassy in London and tried to work it out. We protested vigorously. They told us to go back to our carriage. What a night, trying to sleep.

On the last morning we entered the outskirts of Tehran not knowing what our fate was to be and still without our passports. The police finally came to the door with our passports and, without saying anything, handed them back. The officer who spoke English then came and said it was a national holiday in Tehran and they would celebrate by giving us a pardon.

What a godsend to see those passports and to finally get a good look at the so called "forgery" that had taken place! The passports went back to their safe places. Mine in a pouch around my neck and Pedro's inside his waist band. We weren't impressed by the whole situation and, not surprisingly, we were really angry that they had put us through all that.

DWELLER ON THE THRESHOLD

Once the train stopped we jumped off and made a fast exit to a recommended hotel. All the traveller-style western hotels were grouped in one part of town near the motor garages. It was weird. It was such a shitty end of town. I figured all the "hippie" buses had ended up there for repairs and the locals had started renting rooms. Over the years it became the place where cheaper rooms were convenient and available.

We figured there was safety in numbers so we took a room with four beds. Olga and I shared and the boys had one each. Tehran was a big culture shock. This was the centre of the Islamic world and it felt like we were the only western folk in it. The women were covered head to toe in the burqa with only their eyes appearing through a letterbox hijab veil. The men wore dark jalabiyas or cheap suits. The city was tidy and wealthy compared to other parts of the country. The streets were wide and there were huge squares. It was dry but well-placed trees and gardens softened the landscape. It was a hard place to sight-see as it was so spread out. Buses would have helped but they only displayed Persian signage. We walked until we could no more and headed back to our neighbourhood for a meal.

In our hotel we met some French travellers who had just come back from Afghanistan. We absorbed as much information as we could and, on parting, they gave us a small piece of hash. We were keen to smoke it, but super paranoid. There were signs everywhere saying it was against the law to do drugs.

In the safety of our room we did an Abdul and emptied a cigarette, put a match to the hash until it started to smoulder and then broke it into the tobacco. We then carefully re-filled the cigarette so it looked exactly like one straight out of a packet. We then headed out into the street where we could light it up without the smoke hanging around in our hotel room.

It was dark by now and we walked until the crowd started to thin. We were right to light up but after a lot of fumbling realised we had no matches. Shit! I grabbed the 'ciggie' and hand-signed the first guy I met to see if he had a light. The odds were good because everybody smoked. He produced a match and lit me up. I sucked, held my breath, and nodded thanks as I moved on with Pedro and Olga in tow. By the time we had gone some distance I was busting to cough it up. It was a big hit – the tobacco and the hash. I was spinning, but I carefully passed the 'ciggie' on as we walked. We were very aware about creating a smoke trail and managed to finish it just before getting back to the hotel. Back in the safety of the room we drifted off and forgot the dramas of the past few days on the train.

The next morning we took in some more sights. We saw some amazingly intricate Islamic art and architecture … but the atmosphere in the city was a bit weird. We were really out of place and the people weren't very warm, so we scoped out the bus station and bought tickets to Mashhad for first thing the next day. Mashhad was a border town in the north-east and a full day's bus ride on fairly decent roads. It was a big day of desert landscapes and with the actual border crossing still another 100 miles away we grabbed a hotel room for the night. Again we found a room big enough to sleep us all. We padlocked the door. Everyone carried their own padlock. Some industrial strength, some not worth having. Most hotels did not have locks or keys to their doors. You brought your own.

The next morning we got a mini bus to the border town of Taybad and started the slow journey through Iranian immigration to Afghani immigration and onto another bus bound for Herat. We thought we might get some heat from the Iranians over the "forged" visa dates, but they just stamped our exit and we were out the other side.

We arrived in Herat mid-afternoon and settled into a hotel in the centre of the town. Herat was a small town and the Afghan people came across as pretty friendly. Feeling safer we took separate rooms, settled into an early dinner, and headed off to bed with the sunset.

The next morning Pedro was missing. We thought he must have gone off on an early morning walk but it was eleven am and he hadn't shown up. We were starting to get worried. The hotel manager said he went out the night before and didn't come back. We got really worried and had no idea where to start looking. All of a sudden there he was at the hotel door. It turned out he had spent the night in jail. He had been caught wandering the streets after dark when there was a curfew. He had bought hash and was heading for the town minaret to see the moon rise when the police intercepted him. They found the hash and wanted to know who sold it to him. Pedro refused to say so they pulled out the electric cattle-prod and hit him across the arms with it. Not knowing where they might put the prod next, Pedro agreed to take part in a sting to buy more hash. The buy went down as planned and the cops carted a yelling Afghani youth off to the slammer. Pedro ran after them to beg their mercy and gave the cops twenty dollars (a small fortune) to go easy on the boy. On his way back to the hotel he bought a complete Afghani outfit including the sandals. His intention was to look like one of the locals but the red hair was always going to be a giveaway.

BOM BOM

We stayed in Herat for another day, checking out the markets and understanding just how poor Afghanistan was compared to Iran. There was very little on sale. Not like the thriving marketplaces of Iran and Turkey. This was a mud and block-brick town and there wasn't a lot of vegetation. The Russians were there in large numbers. We thought they were offering aid. Little did we know that it was the start of a ten year war that would send the U.S.S.R. broke.

The Russians backed Afghan President Taraki but his attempts to modernise the country fell foul of the traditional tribes people, and their fundamentalism along with U.S support grew into the Taliban resistance. Those who resisted the Taraki regime were taken prisoner and executed. About two million locals died in this war and millions fled to neighbouring Iran and Pakistan. The guerrilla fighting Taliban eventually won, the Russians retreated, and stupidly years later the U.S. went in.

Our next stop was Kabul but the direct route east was way too dangerous. Afghani rebels had stronghold towns along the way and they didn't like westerners. It was recommended we travel via Kandahar which was a very roundabout route. We had to head south for a day, stay overnight, and then head north for a day. There was no other way.

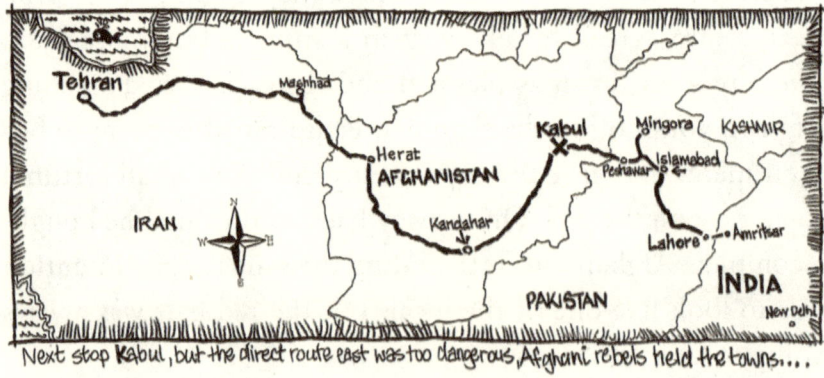

Next stop Kabul, but the direct route east was too dangerous. Afghani rebels held the towns....

DWELLER ON THE THRESHOLD

Bus travel in Afghanistan was interesting. The locals piled into a variety of home-made buses most with bench seats and window openings but no glass. The bodies were timber framed and covered with pressed metal, and they were decorated beyond good taste. They stacked everything on the roof - personal belongings, bedding, building materials, chickens in baskets, goats with their legs tied, everything you could think of. Some people even rode on the top of the bus.

The trip down to Kandahar was amazing. There were camel trains with tribal people and their animals moving across the desert landscape. I couldn't work out whether they were gypsy caravans, people displaced or goat herders on the move. Occasionally there was a mud brick village where, on the street, people sat with guns and watched our bus go by. We hoped they didn't need the target practice especially when we stopped for chai refreshments, lunch and drop toilets. There was a tense mood in the air. Even the locals on the bus didn't feel safe. Sensing the danger we pulled scarfs over our bended heads to try to merge into the scene. At one point we got a flat tyre and had to disembark while the bus crew fixed it. We kept out of sight and huddled in a roadside ditch with the women.

The journey was also an insight into how important trucks were to the country. Everything had to travel by road as there were no railway lines. The trucks, colourfully decorated, were loaded to the hilt and often struggled under the weight. The drivers often had their entire life invested in their truck and as a result they travelled with their families. The trucks, like the buses, were not as we know. Many were built by locals from scratch and had second-hand motors dropped in. The steering, suspension and reliability were suspect and roadside repairs were commonplace.

The drivers were the real heroes as they wrestled their machines in and out of gear, slowed them down, and steered them in traffic, along terrible roads and over mountain passes.

We arrived in Kandahar at nightfall and were ushered to the bus hotel where we were put up for the night. We took a large family room where the five of us bedded down. We secured the room door with my padlock and Troy added his for good measure. There wasn't a lot of talk or sleep that night as the frontier sights from the bus trip played like a picture reel in our heads. We were a long way from anywhere.

The next day we were on the bus at six thirty am and ready for another twelve hour journey. The sights were similar to the day before. Lots of people on the move and lots of guns. We'd managed to pick up a few dry biscuits and some Cokes from the bus station before we left, so we had something to sustain us. It was hot that day and there were few stops along the way.

Coca Cola was pretty much everywhere along this trading route. It was even available on the highest mountain passes. Unless you could boil the water, it was the only safe drink. And sometimes it was even served cold. We tried not to drink too much of it, as it was a lot more expensive than chai, and nowhere near as refreshing.

Late that afternoon we arrived in Kabul. It was an oasis in the desert. Lots of Russian, Chinese and Afghan troops and police. Oblivious to the underlying tensions we checked out the markets, bought local clothes and picked up a few souvenirs. We did our first "scam" in Kabul where we bought Indian rupees on the black market. It was worth doing as we got about thirty percent better value but we didn't exchange too much as we weren't familiar with the rupee notes. Scams or underground transactions became a common activity, especially in currency exchange. Getting a good rate was important as it meant an extra couple of days spending money.

There really wasn't a lot of formality to doing business in this part of the world as most things were done in the street. Someone (which usually meant two or three guys, as they always moved in small groups) would approach you and offer help. You would say "I need a bus ticket" or "I need something to eat", or "I want to buy a coat" or "I want to exchange money". They would then either take you there or one would go off and bring back the person you needed. It just worked.

Our first meal in Kabul was memorable. We had a cheese omelette which was very exotic but it gave us the worst two days of vomiting and diarrhoea we were to experience on the entire trip. Each of us got it as we were sharing a big room. It smelt like rotten egg gas. Thankfully the room was bright and breezy. Whatever airs and graces we might have had were exposed and we could only laugh to fight our way through the stench.

Our days in Kabul were subdued as our sensitive tummies kept us close to the hotel and, with all the uniforms around, it was good to lie low. There were also a lot of other travellers and businessmen and aid workers. There were also lots of Afghan men and definitely no Afghan women. Kabul was a real hub. The bus stations were crowded and it was mayhem. There was no English signage so it was funny to see the westerners yelling at the drivers. The drivers might have known some English or Russian but French, German, Spanish or Japanese was a bridge too far. It was total confusion as they tried to find their rides.

The markets in Kabul were exotic with fantastic woven carpets, blankets, leather goods, brassware and animals. Pedro bought a small brass water pipe. Olga bought a velvet top and I got two small carpet squares.

It was then time to get on a bus to Jalalabad, the next town close to the Pakistan border. I remember the bus was really crowded but we managed to take over the very back bench seat. On the way we shared a big joint, and no one was any the wiser as we blew the smoke out the open back window. After changing buses we arrived at the outpost border crossing at Torkham. It was closed and there was nothing else around. No restaurants or hotels. Just a make shift chai shop with some rope beds beside a mud brick building. The locals were sitting around a big fire. It was quite cold so we joined them to keep warm. They were smoking a large hubble bubble of hashish and they invited us to join in.

There are never a lot of chairs on offer so joining any social group usually meant you had to squat. It was pretty uncomfortable at first. Your back ached and your legs went to sleep, but after a while you got used to it and it ended up being quite a relaxing position. One of the guys crouching around the fire was a very small man dressed in a rough woollen jalabiya and car-tyre rubber sandals covered his brick like feet. His hair, beard and eyes were wild. When his turn came to smoke he balanced himself and wrapped one leg around the pipe. He sucked hard and the pipe came to life. As he sucked he somehow got his other foot around the pipe and, balancing, stood up on it. It was an acrobatic feat. By now he had a flame six inches long coming out of the bowl and he blew out enough smoke to hide in. He was one with the pipe - balancing, sucking and blowing. We had to laugh as he looked like a genie coming out of the hubble bubble. Eventually the bowl was empty and he climbed off to lie by the fire to recover.

These guys were serious smokers. They had three or four lumps of local hash on a piece of cardboard by the pipe. Each piece was about twenty grams and looked like it had been hand-rubbed into a poo-sized dropping. Pedro added a small piece of his stash and the locals sniffed at it and talked enthusiastically about its quality. By the time the hubble bubble had been around the ring a couple of times the hash was pretty much gone.

In reality the hash was only one part of the stone. The tobacco was the another. It was rough and potent. Often grown in the same fields as the poppies and marijuana, there was no processing, it was simply dried, cut and smoked.

With a head full of zombie we curled up on our gear and slept lightly whilst resting our over-travelled bodies. Sunrise came and one by one our newfound friends left. It was really cold so we stoked up the fire, and before long the chai baba took over and started handing out hot tea with concentrated tinned milk. Embracing the sun, we took in the landscape, imagining those that had travelled through there over the past few thousand years. The camel and horse trains from yesteryear were now truck trains that lined up for miles on either side of the border.

At seven in the morning the timber doors to the mud brick building opened. We were among the first through and inside we met our camp-fire hosts from the previous evening. They were now in their old beaten and dirty immigration and customs overcoats. We were a little taken aback, and wondered where this was going to go, as they knew that we were holding. They laughed as they looked through our passports and, with a smile and wave of the arm, they ushered us through the final doorway. On the other side were Pakistani officials and a mini bus that was to take us through the Khyber Pass.

We'd heard a lot about the thousand-metre-high Khyber Pass corridor that connected Afghanistan and Pakistan. It had originally been a part of the Silk Road that connected Shanghai to Cadiz on the south west coast of Spain. It had been the scene of battles for thousands of years as the conquering armies of warriors like Genghis Khan moved west and it was where Muslim invaders moved east to India. Although it was on the Pakistani side, no government owned the Khyber. It was run by local tribesmen and war lords. It was no man's land and the locals knew it.

The bus conductor was a nervous twenties-something guy who checked our tickets carefully. I figured he needed glasses. The driver was older, had red eyes and looked stoned out of his head. There were two men sitting in the roof rack with rifles.

Troy decided we needed a big joint to calm our nerves and after the bus got moving he lit it up. There was a lot of smoke in the cabin so the conductor tried to get us to stop. No one was taking any notice. Some of the other hippie passengers also got the urge to stoke up, and before long there were joints being passed everywhere. The conductor was freaking and opening windows to get fresh air. But the driver didn't flinch, he was focused and taking deep breaths whenever he could.

The bus moved very quickly, oversteering into the downhill corners and getting way too close to the edge of the ravine. It took a few hours to wind our way down and along the Khyber Khwar river valley and back up the other side. The uphill stretch was tighter and a lot slower and there were times when it was way too slow to be comfortable.

DWELLER ON THE THRESHOLD

Throughout the fifty-mile trip we saw small groups of people on the move ... and all had guns. A few times we were stopped at checking stations by riflemen. The bus driver paid a toll. These slow downs were a good chance to see historic British fortifications, Christian, Hindu and Muslim memorials and headstones going back centuries. It was special ... and spooky. The driver had given us a "no photographs" warning before we started the trip, so unfortunately my camera was in my backpack.

Once at the top of the valley we knew we were safe. We'd run the gauntlet - no ambush and no going off the edge. The bus stopped at a small village called Jamrud, where we had a chai and, with nothing else to see, we boarded a bigger bus for Peshawar.

Peshawar was another border town. Except it was big and super populated. I remember stepping off the bus and almost treading on an old rag in the gutter which turned out to be a begging woman. This town was like stepping into a time warp. If it wasn't for the traffic and the spaghetti maze of overhead power lines it could have been two thousand years earlier. No one wore western clothing. The timber shops housed tailors, cobblers, horse stables and restaurants. They were all a throwback to another time.

This was a Muslim town. It was crazy. No sophisticated Iranians, no proud Afghanis, just Pakistanis all trying to eke out some sort of living. We ended up in a fairly decent hotel for the town. Separate rooms. Olga and I shared, but soon got the feeling we were being watched. On careful inspection we found the walls of the room were peppered with tiny holes and there was a pair of eyes in each.

I couldn't believe it and quickly opened the door to see half a dozen men scatter down the corridor. I then spent an hour plugging the holes with wet paper plugs only to have them pushed out within seconds. In the end we were resigned to the fact that we were going to be on display so we hung some sheets around the bed.

Troy had been told of an opium den down the street from the hotel. The next day we went to check it out. The guy that took us led us through a maze of little streets and into a doorway. I tried to look for landmarks along the way but it was hard. The den was dark and it had a very strong smell about it. There were a number of rope beds which we were ushered to. There was one other customer asleep on a bed. He was a local. We lay there watching the ceremony of the old pipe master melting down the hard opium and working it onto a bamboo stick and holding it to the end of the pipe. He lit this with a taper from an oil lamp and each of us had a turn sucking up the smoke or as the Chinese call it 'chasing the dragon'.

To smoke you laid on a mat in front of him with a brick block as a pillow. Pretty uncomfortable at first but after the first pipe you didn't feel a thing. No wonder opiates are used to mask pain. Once you had a turn you got up and returned to your bed to experience the high. We had about three pipes each and were totally gone. It was a very different high. Your lungs were warm, your stomach queazy, and there was a bucket close by if you needed to vomit. It was a cloudy, dreamlike experience and your limbs became very heavy. After some hours of drifting in and out of sleep we somehow mustered enough strength, agreed to leave, and stumbled our way through the laneways and passages that led to our hotel. I don't know how we did it but I think it had something to do with following the noise to the main street.

The next morning we gathered at breakfast. We ordered but didn't eat anything. We just spent the time talking about the den. Troy and Ryan were keen to go back. Pedro and Olga were with them, so I went along for the ride. Same ceremony as the day before, except this time while we were lying in dreamtime the cops came in. For a brief second I was expecting a drama and then I didn't care. The cops had a look around, counted the bodies and after a short chat with the owner left clutching a bunch of backhander rupees. Sometime during this session a chai boy came in and provided hot sugared tea which we sipped into consciousness.

Again we got out unscathed and, after sleeping it off, we went out to check out the town. There were gun shops where anyone could buy all sorts of pistols, rifles, ammo and scimitar knives. Some of it looked like military issue and some were blunderbusses from the past. There were chemist shops that sold cocaine, heroin, morphine, mandrax, quaaludes and other assorted pharmaceuticals that were banned or withdrawn from sale in the west. It was a dumping ground. You could buy anything openly in this town … except alcohol as it was against their religion. It was the wild frontier. A lot of opium passed through this town on its way to or from Afghanistan.

On one of our outings Olga and I met a cobbler who invited us to chai and to see his backroom operation. It was Shoe Making 101 from the pre-industrial revolution. He spoke a little bit of English and invited us to a country wedding the next day. When our hotel owners found out what we were doing they warned us off going with anyone into the countryside.

Next morning the boys went to the opium den while Olga and I went back to the cobbler's shop where a car took us out of the town and into the countryside. We entered a walled compound where the wedding was to take place. There was some sort of party planned but we didn't see either the bride or the groom. There was just a lot of men sitting around on rope beds in the yard. There were rifles all over the place. We started to get seriously worried and remembered the hotel owner's warning.

For a while all was calm and in simple English we told them we were from Australia and we talked about kangaroos which they seemed to get. We'd learnt earlier that coming from the U.S.A. didn't go down well in a lot of places. Then one of the guys picked up his rifle and started firing at the wall. The noise reverberated off the walls and scared the shit out of us. Olga grabbed my hand and we quietly slid off the bed looking for an escape route. The rifleman then turned and motioned for me to stay. He then handed me the gun and indicated I should have a few shots. Boy was I glad to get that gun in my hands. Both Olga and I had a few shots. The noise and recall of the butt were something else. Relieved we handed the gun back and then out came the hubble bubble and food and eventually the bride and groom arrived. It turned out to be a great day and very insightful. We tasted some fabulous sweets, drank tea, smoked and laughed. When it was time to go the men shot their guns into the sky as we got back in the car and headed down the road and back into town.

The wedding guests told us that the best hashish in the world came from Chitral which was high in the Hindu Kush mountains and close to Afghanistan. We wanted to go there but it was still too early in the season and the passes were closed. Instead we decided to head up the Swat Valley which was pretty much directly north of our current location. It was not as high up, so there was not a lot of snow around.

I was keen to leave as soon as possible as the boys and Olga were getting way too familiar with the opium den and they were starting to become obsessed by the high. That night at dinner the boys weren't interested in the food and nodded off mid-conversation. I said we were leaving next day but I wasn't sure they heard me. The next morning Olga and I went around to their rooms early. They were still asleep and didn't want to go. It was also Pedro's birthday and he had other ideas on how he wanted to celebrate. They were also still quite out of it and told us to bugger off. I was very keen to at least get Olga and Pedro on the bus. Troy and Ryan could really do as they liked. We managed to pack them all up, got them dressed, paid their hotel bills and pushed them to the bus stop. Despite their protests they knew they didn't want to be left behind.

I bought the tickets and the driver held up the departure while Troy, Ryan and Pedro fluffed around getting tea and cakes, stowing their gear and climbing the steps of the bus. There was lots of yelling from the conductor, the passengers and the driver. I knew what it was all about. They wanted to get moving and the hippies were holding them up. I wanted to distance myself from the group so I grabbed Olga and we climbed up onto the roof rack amongst the luggage. We made ourselves comfortable and settled in for the ride of our lives.

The bus climbed slowly and the roads got thinner and more rugged as we worked our way up the river valley. It was amazing being on the roof of the bus and seeing the vista around us. The river raged with the spring-melted snow. It was wild. Huge volumes of water tearing through the river gorges, unsettling boulders the size of cars and tearing away at the valley walls. I could imagine the road in front of us being snatched away by the water and was a bit uneasy as we moved forward. The only good thing about being on the roof was that if the bus fell into the ravine we could leap off without being crushed inside. An interesting thought.

The bus stopped three times during the trip. Chai huts and a lunchtime truck stop. The locals were mostly farmers on horseback or goat herders. We were definitely on the outer fringe of life as we knew it.

Later that day we stopped in Mingora, a frontier town in the valley. We found a place to stay the night and went exploring. We came across a government-run opium and hashish shop selling local produce. There were a few locals in the shop ahead of us buying small chunks for their evening enjoyment. We had bigger things in mind and we each bought a tola (ten grams) of nice black hash. Troy bought a tola of opium as well, which over the next week or so, he ate piece by piece. I was happy when the others decided to just smoke and keep clear of the 'OP'.

We then found a restaurant and had a vegetable and rice dish with a chai, and it was back to the hotel. On the way we were treated to a chorus of noisy cuckoo birds. What an amazing soundscape as we walked up the narrow tree lined road. What an amazing sunset view of the mountain range and … a full moon. It was magic.

The hotel owner grabbed me on arrival and started to proposition me about buying Olga. Pedro was with me and we laughed. He thought we were laughing at the price. So he got really serious and upped the ante from four to six goats. I tried to be consoling and said she was my wife. That was the end of it. I told Olga who was disappointed she was only worth six goats. I told her they had golden fleece.

The accommodation was strange. It was like a big dorm room with lots of beds. Come nightfall we all had to be in our room because there was a curfew. Apparently the hills men came into town at night and the police were there to keep the peace. Given there was no alcohol, I figured the hills men were more likely to be stoned, harmless and just looking for something to do.

There were big timber gates sealing the hotel off from the street. The owner then came around and padlocked our room door so we couldn't get out. In turn we padlocked it to make sure he couldn't get in. Now there we were. It was twelve hours before we could get back out again. It felt a bit like being in jail. There were three or four other travellers in the room so we all put our hash on the table and started with chillums and card games. This went on through the night as we told stories of our adventures.

One story that freaked us out was the one about Jean-Jacque and Dirty Pierre. The two French junkies who befriended, and then murdered, other travellers to get money and buy drugs. They travelled under false passports to avoid being captured by Interpol. It sounded a lot like the Charles Sobhraj story we had been following in the local papers. Not a lot of sleep that night given a few of the other freaks we were sharing with were French, and they wee the ones who had brought up the stories. I had a decent size knife in my pack and I made sure it was unsheathed and in my sleeping bag.

The next morning we got up with the sun. We went to find a bus to take us further up the Swat Valley. We had entered an intensely beautiful area. A rich flood plain valley, surrounded by snow-capped mountains, full of opium poppies in bloom. The valley was awash in purple colour. Once again we managed to get a place on top of the bus among the chickens and goats and baskets. It was a fantastic trip as the old bus pottered along the skinny roads through the small villages.

We arrived in Kalokot about lunchtime and found a funny timber hotel that was built out over the river. It was mad. There was a raging river running under the hotel and the noise was so loud you couldn't hear a thing. After a while it became really peaceful as the sound drowned everything from your mind and you were left in a higher place. We stayed there for a week. It was very cheap. The food was good (rice plus something for every meal) and the tea was perfumed and refreshing. It was there we met an old Pakistani guy working in a chai shop. He was such a beautiful person. Always smiling. He had a crescent moon and star tattoo on his forehead. He said he got it in prison. I wasn't sure if the prisoners were identified that way, or whether he got it to show he was a part of some group or perhaps as a symbol of his Islamic faith.

We took some great walks in the countryside through the opium and marijuana fields. It was fascinating getting a close-up view of opium harvesting and hash making.

To harvest the opium the farmers would cut a small slice on the side of the seed pod and it bled a rubbery sap that was scraped into a bag. This was heated into a goo that could be worked into a putty that went hard. This could then be heated to be smoked or chemically processed to become heroin, morphine or codeine.

The marijuana farmers on the other hand would harvest their marijuana at the end of summer and process the seeds, buds and leaves to make oil, hashish and smoking kif. The stalks were stripped to become fibre and rope. Some harvested an early hash (charas) by walking through the fields in a leather apron. The pollen from the flowering heads would stick and at the end of the day they scraped it off, and hand-worked it into a putty which they would heat and add to their hubble bubble mix.

The hotel manager didn't really like us venturing too far as it was a dangerous frontier town and lots of tribal folk were wandering around. He thought we would be robbed at the very least, but we had nothing of any value on us as our passports and money were in the hotel safe. Regardless we kept within a running radius of the hotel.

During my time in Kalokot I read, drank tea and smoked joints. From 6am till 9pm we all followed this routine. Everyone contributed to smoko. The joints were rolled using three to five cigarette papers, mimicking the spliffs of Jamaica. A cardboard filter gave the joint structure so it could be held between the fingers in a closed fist for hygiene reasons.

Reading was a great way to pass the time. Book swaps were big and you had a great choice in every hotel lobby where it was common to "leave one and take one". My mind was opened to a lot of things. A few of my memorable reads were -

Robert Pirsig's *Zen and the Art of Motorcycle Maintenance* which was the story of keeping a motorcycle going while on a very long journey and the numerous *philosophical* thoughts it engendered. I loved motorcycles so I probably gleaned more than most from this one.

The Tibetan Book of the Dead, originally written by Padmasambhava in the 1300s, it describes the experiences of the consciousness in the interval between death and the next *rebirth*. Great background to deciphering some of the Tibetan circle of life artworks I was exposed to later on.

Herman Hesse's *Siddhartha, Steppenwolf* and *The Glass Bead Game*, beautiful stories which explore an individual's search for *authenticity*, self-knowledge and *spirituality*. If you haven't read *Siddhartha* you really should. It's a short book with a wonderful story. It is on par with *The Pilgrimage* and *The Alchemist* by Paulo Coelho.

Carlos Castaneda's books – *A Separate Reality* and *Journey to Ixtlan* – which describe his peyote mind-expanding experiences and training in shamanism under Don Juan Matus, a *Yaqui* "Man of Knowledge".

Autobiography of a Yogi, the life of Paramahansa Yogananda and his encounters with spiritual figures from both the East and West. Great insights from his childhood, finding his guru, becoming a monk and establishing his own teachings on Kriya Yoga meditation. The book is an introduction to attaining God-realisation - after reading this I was ready for India.

And then there were the classics which I had somehow missed out on - Dostoyevsky's *Crime and Punishment*, Oscar Wilde's *The Picture of Dorian Gray*, F. Scott Fitzgerald's *The Great Gatsby*, Doris Lessing's *The Grass is Singing*.

These were all great books to prepare one for the spirituality of India. They opened my mind to meditation as a way of stilling the mind and the clarity that comes with this. I was initially very sceptical about gurus and religion as I had been brought up as a Catholic and attended a Christian school where they were anything but Christian. I subsequently became a non-believer and took more from my *Don't Worry Be Happy* Meher Baba poster that was hung in my bedroom shortly after my first joint. I wanted to be my own guru and loved Frank Zappa's perception in his song *Cosmic Debris*.

There was lots of smoking and the hotel was pretty easy about us doing it in their public spaces. On one of our walks we came across the town's Government Hash and Opium Shop. It wasn't hard to find as there was a sign above the entrance. There was a big man sitting on the porch and inside there was a small blind albino guy. He stood out from everyone else. As a sign of respect we wished them peace, "As-Salaam-alykum". This could be shortened to be a simple "Salaam" hello. We asked to buy some hashish. The big guy had followed us in to oversee the proceedings. The blind man reached for a drawer under the counter in front of him and pulled out three or four chunks. They were different grades, so he bit off a small piece from each block and lit each with a candle so we could smell the aroma.

None of the chunks looked very black so we made stamping signs. The big guy muttered something and the little guy pulled out the 00 primo grade. The one with the gold stamp. Our eyes lit up. We thought we'd just get a tola each until he told us the price was about $2.50. It didn't take long to figure we should get enough to last a while. We asked for two hundred and fifty grams each. It was nice small block and easy enough to stash. The blind guy measured and weighed each on the scales like he could see what he was doing. He was amazing, he knew exactly how much things weighed just by handling them. And if they were short he would just bite off another piece to balance it out. We tried not to think about what might be in his saliva. We were going to burn it anyway.

We were in the final stages of settling up when a hills man came into the room. He was carrying a rifle like most did. He chatted in Urdu for a while, and then lifted his robe. He had about ten kilos of hash wrapped around his body. We just watched in amazement as he kept unravelling and pulling out bricks of hash. He was obviously a "market gardener" bringing in his produce. He collected a roll of notes from the big guy and left.

Apparently government hash and opium stores were legal in the valleys but moving the crop down into the towns and cities was illegal. So there were a lot of police outposts along the roads checking horses and trucks coming down from the hills. The opium and marijuana crops were very important to the local people. They were the only crops they could grow successfully in the short summer season and their whole existence was geared to it. It was also the perfect crop to help pass the time when your house was buried in snow for six months of the year.

The government knew of the drug's economic importance so they taxed it and in some cases became the wholesaler for it. The government was getting a lot of pressure from the Americans and others to restrict the trade as a lot of the opium harvest ultimately made its way to the United States and Europe as heroin. It was a confusing situation for the locals.

So now we each had a personal stash and it was time to head back down the valley and make our way through Islamabad, Rawalpindi and then to Lahore the next big Pakistani city before India. The bus ride down was another mind-blowing experience. All of us managed to get in amongst the luggage on the roof so we had a panoramic view all the way down the valley. It didn't take long for the chillum to be passed around so we really got to appreciate the journey and its surroundings.

Islamabad and Rawalpindi were really hard work. The locals were friendly but these were really crowded towns and the infrastructure was basic. We moved as quickly as we could. On arrival in Lahore we felt like we were on another planet. It was crazy. Pakistani men are on heat most of the time but in a big city, with the women in hiding, they were outrageous. With nothing to lose they hassled Olga. I found out why she kept knitting needles in her duffle bag. If anyone touched her, she jabbed them with some force. It was no fun being a white woman in Lahore.

Troy on the other hand was having a ball as he entertained a small group of young men in his room. He was like a Cheshire Cat sitting around in his jalabaya, rolling joints and sending his boys on errands. I could only imagine what else he was getting up to.

One morning Olga and I came down to reception and the manager grabbed us and said there was an English girl Olga should meet. She agreed and he knocked on the door of a room. It was answered by a small blonde who was visibly upset and when she saw it was another white girl she invited us in. Her name was Julia and she had been invited to Pakistan by a female pen-friend who turned out to be a rich guy who kept her locked up for sex. He even prostituted her out to others. He had taken all her money and passport so she had nowhere to go. Things must have been getting too hot for him, so he dropped her in the city with her passport and drove off. Our hotel was close, so she asked if they had somewhere where she could sleep. She was a mess and at a loss as to what to do next.

With little option, and with a slight inkling we were being scammed, we took her to the closest airline shop and bought her a Pakistan International Airlines ticket to Karachi with a connection on to London. There was a flight leaving the next day so we spent the rest of the day with her as she recounted her horrible story. She was treated like a dog and was probably scarred for life as a result. I was pretty angry but knew it was a waste of time going to the police. Julia was so thankful and didn't know how to repay us. She gave Olga a small jade pendant.

Our group had travelled together for a number of months now, but we were starting to splinter. We got on well together, but Pakistan was just too tough. Troy and Ryan wanted to head back to the States so they made arrangements to fly out. Pedro was getting low on funds so he was keen to move quickly to India and on to Bangkok so he could get a flight back to Australia. It wasn't quite the original plan that we hatched in London where we would go overland from Bangkok to Malaysia, Singapore, Indonesia, Bali, Darwin and work our way back home. But this one made sense given the circumstances.

Amazingly Troy and Ryan were on the same flight out as Julia so we all went to the airport to say goodbye. We were glad the boys were accompanying Julia to make sure she got on the plane. And we had lots of laughs in the coffee shop recounting our adventures. As Pedro, Olga and I watched them board we knew we too were ready to leave. A lot of people we met called us infidels and were quite aggressive. Apparently the Koran said anyone who didn't believe in Allah was fair game. I think what they all really needed was a drink and a good root. They were obviously repressed beyond religion.

In the past Pakistani life wasn't always as rigorous as it was when we passed through the country. When the British ruled over India the Muslim and Hindu societies were integrated and, although there were issues, they accepted each other's beliefs and got on with life. It was a balanced society. When the British left in 1947 they set Pakistan up as an independent state to split the two religions and the wall between beliefs got bigger. There was a lot of ethnic cleansing on both sides. Unfortunately, Pakistan remained in a void under British rule until 1956 when it finally became the Islamic Republic of Pakistan. Whereas India had those nine years to shape its future under Mohandas Gandhi, who became Mahatma (Great Soul) Gandhi as he peacefully changed government and society.

As life went on those Muslims who remained in India settled into a peaceful existence. They had their beliefs and there were mosques everywhere to unite their communities. Their Hindu brothers were believers in Dharma which was the righteous way, and they had enough gods on their side to encourage a life of peace. They also believed that the soul is immortal and would be reborn in a better place if they lived an honourable life according to the Bhagavada Gita, the sacred scriptures.

With Troy and Ryan's departure, and thoughts for poor Julia, we made our way to the border as quickly as we could. It was late afternoon when we arrived and it was really hot. We weren't wearing a lot of clothes, so it was hard to hide anything. Pedro and I had our stash from Kalokot and the blackmarket Indian rupees from Afghanistan in our backpacks. Olga had hers and Troy and Ryan's leftovers in her sari waist-band. Getting through Pakistani Customs was easy enough. Then there was about a kilometre walk through no man's land in the heat before we came to the Indian outpost.

We had heard stories and read (on the University notice board in London) about an Indian customs woman who claimed to be a psychic. And there she was, poppy-eyed and resplendent in a silk sari. Apparently, she could look you in the eye and know if you were carrying drugs. I thought it was all very funny, and had trouble holding back a friendly giggle as she stared at me and tried to vibe me out. Thankfully she waved me through. Next Olga lined up for her piercing mug shot and she got through. It was then Pedro's turn to stare her down. He must have tried too hard because she picked up on something and asked him to empty his shoulder bag which she fingered through with a pencil. She then pointed at his backpack while she went off to stare someone else down.

Halfway through his unpack Pedro pulled out a cricket ball that he had picked up in Pakistan. The Indian customs guys who were standing nearby asked if he was in the Australian team. Pedro's personality lit up. He became the good guy as he laughed and talked enthusiastically about the players whom they all knew well - Thomson, Lillee, Marsh, Chappell. Pedro was stalling. India - Gavaskar and Ali, now he had them in raptures. Meanwhile another official turned up and spoke to the team. He waved at the clock which read a few minutes to five pm which was closing time. The psychic looked back at a half-unpacked Pedro and pencil-waved him through. What a relief! Close one Pedro. We all had a nervous and relieved laugh as we walked out of the building. For some time after Pedro would often stare at me with poppy-eyes when he wanted to make a comment about the absurdity of a situation. I would always respond with a stare and a smile.

India, what an amazing land! The smell was different. Perhaps it was helped by the rows of roses lining the path out to the bus terminal. The people were colourful and vibrant. Unlike Pakistan, there were women everywhere and there was flesh showing. Arms and midriffs - enough to corrupt a man. No wonder the Indians and Pakistanis have such a tenuous relationship. It's got to be all about sex! One was getting it, the other wasn't.

The landscape in front of us was expansive. Roads were going in all directions. We felt like we had been following a one-lane track for the past few months and now we could choose any direction we wanted. The closest city was Amritsar so we grabbed the next bus out. The music on the radio was different. Upbeat, over-produced Bollywood songs. And it was loud. We were across the top ten songs before arriving in Amritsar and were walking into the Golden Temple with jingles in our heads. The temple was huge, and despite being built in 1604 by the Sikhs, it looked like it was new.

Sikhism was founded in the Punjab region of India in the fifteenth century by Guru Nanak Dev, who broke away from Hinduism because of its caste system and his belief in only one immortal being called God. The Sikhs were proud warriors and known as the 'Lions of the Punjab'. They were also well-travelled and clever merchants. Initiated Sikhs would cover uncut hair with a tight turban, carry the Kirpan sword, wear a steel bracelet, and for personal hygiene they wore under garments and carried a wooden comb.

The Golden Temple was open to all pilgrims. You could refresh, have a meal and bed-down for the night. And it was free. It was also a cool place to shelter from the blistering heat. We found a cool marble corner inside the building and stowed our gear. We showered fully clothed and within minutes were dry again. We then joined hundreds of other pilgrims for a

BOM BOM

meal in a cool covered area in the middle of a large ornamental lake. When a space became available you sat cross-legged on the ground until the line of devotees passed ladling food out onto one's banana leaf. It was really clean and tasty and there was plenty of it.

Throughout history the Golden Temple wasn't without conflict. In 1984 the Indian police and army attacked the Temple to remove some militant Sikhs who were hiding in the building. The army were disrespectful, they damaged the temple and killed pilgrims. Later that year Indian Prime Minister Indira Gandhi was assassinated by her Sikh bodyguards. An eye for an eye, in good Sikh style.

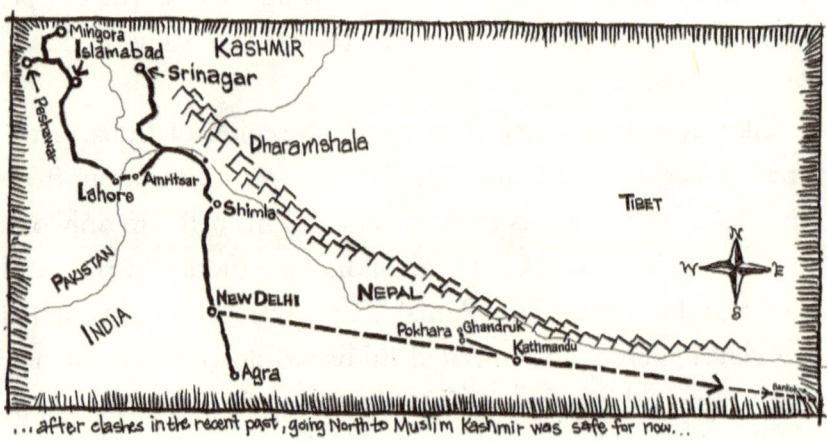

...after clashes in the recent past, going North to Muslim Kashmir was safe for now...

We spent a few days exploring Amritsar which was on another level compared to previous cities. A sensory onslaught of sound, colour and activity. We were lucky to be invited to join a wedding party as it made its way through the streets. It was a parade complete with elephants and bands and dancing, and the food at the end was a spectacular feast. We hadn't seen so much great looking, assorted, colourful food in all our travels.

DWELLER ON THE THRESHOLD

After a few days in the temple we regained our strength and decided to head north to Kashmir where it was cooler. When the British left India, they made Muslim Kashmir a part of India, and there have been clashes with Muslim separatists ever since. It was quiet for now, so we felt safe making our way up to the region. Pedro wasn't sure if he should go because of the dwindling funds but we convinced him to come along.

We left Amritsar and bussed it across the desert plains to Pathankot, and then north on to the foothills of Jammu for the night. The landscape was changing with lots more trees and the temperature had dropped slightly. Jammu was a hill-side trading town. There were a lot of people and their animals on the street. The goats and sheep were noisy but stuck close to their shepherds. The holy cows were something else. Some were huge brahmans and they had free-reign. They went where they wanted, and ate what they wanted, until the locals shoo'ed them off. They did contribute something as they were the garbage sweepers, who cleaned up everything in their path. And when they made a mess, the poorer folk quickly scooped up their huge fibre filled patties which were dried and burnt for warmth and cooking. They had massive horns so most people gave them a wide berth. One day in a tight squeeze I got too close to one of these beasts and it threw its head sideways into my shoulder. It knocked me off my feet and I had a bruised shoulder and arm for months afterwards.

We left Jammu the next morning on a twelve-hour bus ride. There were a few stops but not the best places to take a dump. The toilets were absolutely rank. Basically drop downs that had overflowed and if you were lucky there was a tap or stream close by to wash yourself. Toilet paper wasn't in the mix. If there was any, you were carrying it and then you had to think about how you were going to dispose of it. Mostly you used your left hand and water provided to clean yourself. It was an art that the locals perfected over a lifetime. Early in the piece we learnt that you sat on your left hand when eating – it helped to eliminate any accidental interaction with your food. It was an insult to use that hand at mealtime. One extreme civil criminal punishment was to cut the left hand off so the right hand had to be used for everything. You became a social outcast for life.

The roads changed as we headed up into the Himalayas. They became tighter and tighter the higher we went until they were just a built-up wedge on the side the mountain. It was crazy how many trucks and buses used that "track". One lane … but carrying two directions of traffic. I am not sure if the Indians were having fun but the roadside signs were almost comic, one in particular read "Watch My Curves" and was stencilled over a female silhouette, it always got the driver's attention.

Some vehicles went over the edge when trying to pass or when backing up to let another vehicle through. And when the weather was bad the road just collapsed. At various points along the road we had to wait for them to fix a washout before we could proceed. It was frightening and scary looking back and seeing three of four tyre tracks behind the bus. The other one was floating over the edge and into oblivion.

The road got to a point where it couldn't go any higher, it was two thousand two hundred metres. Then the bus swung right burying itself into the Jawahar Tunnel. For the next three kilometres we travelled through the mountain. It was built for light two-way jeep-style traffic in 1956 but had since become an essential trading route for trucks and buses. It was over-used and crumbling everywhere. It was dark, wet and there was barely enough room to pass. The drivers had to pull their wing mirrors in. You could see into the cabins of the vehicles travelling in the opposite direction.

It was a slow crawl through the rough-sawn rock but once we emerged it was an amazing feeling. Like being born again. The sun was shining. It was cool, the roads were good, and the bus rolled effortlessly along the ridges as it worked its way down into the valley. We passed through willow groves and towns where they were making cricket bats. Thousands of them leaning up against trees like a strange roadside fence. After a few more stops, and a very sore backside, we arrived in Srinagar in the late afternoon. It was impressively beautiful and worth the ride. An ornate timber town built around a large lake system, surrounded by snow-capped mountain ranges which were reflected in the blue sky water.

We had heard that the best place to stay was on a houseboat on Dal Lake, so we found a tout who got a paddle boat and showed us a few of the craft that were available to rent. They were amazing. They ranged from triple-story English gin palaces to more traditional long boats. All were carved timber and impressively ornate. We picked a large long boat and passed our gear on to a teen helper who showed us aboard and introduced the cook.

It was really, really cold on the lake so we were given woollen capes and a small wicker basket which held a clay bowl filled with hot coals. This we held under our capes. The little fellas were quickly warmed but the other extremities were as cold as ice. The next day there was a constant flow of boats visiting to sell fruit, vegetables, carpets, wooden carvings, and other essential items. We bought a hubble bubble and some local black hash and sat smoking on the boat's deck while we watched the clouds paint the sky.

If you wanted, you could hail a canoe or something larger to take you to any place on the lake. On one trip we found a fur shop and I couldn't resist an otter skin hat. It was beautiful and the warmest thing you could imagine. Our "taxi" paddlers were always keen to show us a family or a friend's handicraft factory which was built on the shores or floated on the lake. We bought a few small pieces, including a carpet, which took four days to negotiate the price. There was a lot of tea drinking and we learnt lots about what makes a good carpet. In the end the carpet, some paper-mache and wooden boxes, and some extraneous clothing were sent from the Srinagar post office back home to Sydney.

Going to the post office was a three to four-hour chore. You needed to come prepared to weigh the goods, put them in a cardboard box, tape it, wrap the box in calico cloth, stitch the cloth with a needle and thread, tie the box with string, get a marker pen to write the address and sender all over it, and take it - and the completed customs paperwork - back to the queue for the appropriate stamps, seals and payment. I later learnt the parcels took six weeks to arrive but they did arrive.

Somewhere on the lake we met Rasool Jon. He had the best hashish. Black and oily. He wanted to send a load of it to Sydney. Pedro's watch was to be the deposit. The rest could be paid once his wooden boxes lined with the hash arrived in Australia. We paddled over to his brother's box factory to see how it all worked. We then sent a letter-gram to our friend Rod in Sydney to tell him we had some parcels coming his way. We knew he was sympathetic as he was saving for his flight to Delhi so he could meet up. Hopefully this would get him travelling a bit quicker. We had no idea how it was going to work but it sounded like a good thing.

DWELLER ON THE THRESHOLD

Srinagar was the place for our next bout of the shits. All water was pulled from the lake, and the lake was the garbage and excrement dumping ground. Simple arithmetic. We took Lomatil and tried to settle our stomachs by eating yoghurt and just drinking black tea. It lasted for two of the seven days we were aboard. In the end it was just too cold so we decided to move on.

We would have gone north to Leh in Ladakh but the pass was snowed over. Many years later I was lucky to return to Kashmir with my school mate "Wheelie" Paul and we tried once more to go by road from Srinagar to Leh but it was snowed in again. We ended up flying in to Leh which probably wasn't a smart decision, as landing in a place that was 3,500 metres above sea level really plays havoc with your breathing. We spent the first two days lying on a bed with hearts racing trying to acclimatise to the oxygen levels.

Leh was a very Tibetan town built on what seemed like a crater on the moon. It was so rocky and barren. Only the prayer flags provided any colour, but the locals were very accommodating and we stayed with a family in a large one-roomed house. Accommodation was on the first floor. The animals lived on the ground floor and the long drop toilet was a hole in the floor to the animals below. It would have been pretty cosy in there during the long winter months.

With Leh not an option on this trip, Delhi was our next destination. So back on the bus again for the long trip out of the valley, through the mountain tunnel and down the other side. We weren't looking forward to it at all but thankfully we came across a Shiva devotee, a Sadhu, camped in tree roots near the bus stop. After some small chat he stoked up a chillum pipe and we saluted Shiva with a 'Bom Bom Shanka' to prepare us for the journey. The Hindus believed that the mere utterance of Shiva's name would offer protection and eliminate any bad vibes, so we received his blessing and left him beaming in delight with a nice little chunk of Rasool Jon's hash. The long bus trip became a repeat of the initial experience … except in reverse. It was so good to get out of that tunnel, down those skinny roads and onto "ground level" India.

This time when we arrived at Pathankot we caught a bus to the foothill town of Dharmsala in search of the fourteenth Dalai Lama. Tenzin Gyatso was born in 1935 and at the age of two was recognised as the re-incarnation of the previous Dalai Lama. When he was five he entered monastic education and very quickly proved to be a gifted and loving person. His whole "reason for being" was to help humanity. In 1954 at age nineteen, he visited Mao Zedong in Beijing to present his case for a free Tibet. Five years later he escaped the forced Chinese occupation of Tibet and set up his monastic community at McLeod Ganj outside of Dharmsala in India. A lot of Tibetans followed him there and it soon became a Tibetan town.

We took a large room on the hillside for a week and ventured out each day to visit the monastery where we learnt a lot about Buddhism and how to use those principles in daily life. When we weren't at the ashram we were sitting on the hillside overlooking an incredible view that stretched from the Himachal Pradesh range right down to the plains of India hundreds of miles away.

We bought some excellent Manali hash which tasted like meadow flowers and we enjoyed the full moon and listening to an American guy learning to play sitar. We particularly enjoyed it when his teacher was playing. We also enjoyed exploring the forested hills but didn't venture too deep as we had seen the bear, leopard and wolf pelts in the market.

DWELLER ON THE THRESHOLD

We mostly shopped for produce and cooked our own meals. We also ate the hottest curry ever. I should have known better as I saw them make it from scratch. I had never seen so much chilli, curry powder, garlic, onions and roots, leaves and vegetables tossed together in a burning mix of ghee. My eyes were watering just watching from 10 feet away. A mouthful was all I could take. I splashed out, bought a cold Coke and slammed it down to ease the burn. I followed that with a fresh lassi yoghurt drink and a hot chai which almost got rid of the heat.

Unfortunately, the Dalai Lama didn't appear while we were there but we spoke with a number of westerners who had been there for months and they described some of their audiences. I particularly liked one of his quotes "Let us try to recognise the precious nature of each day". From then on, every morning I tried to remind myself of it.

We were aware that we were close to Rishikesh and the Maharishi Mahesh Yogi's ashram but it would have taken us the best part of a week to get to and from it. It was situated in the foothills further east and we would have had to have gone down to the plains of India and then headed back up into the mountains. Too many bus trips. It would have been nice to have done a Transcendental Meditation Course and visited The Beatles ashram where they wrote the *White Album,* but it was just too hard. So Pedro, Olga and I headed down to Delhi via Shimla.

Shimla was an old British colonial town where they retreated to escape the summer heat of the plains. You could just imagine them dressed to the nines while sipping a gin and tonic on the veranda. From Shimla we took the train south to Kalka. It seemed all we did was travel through tunnels. The railway line was an amazing engineering feat - most of it had been dug and laid by hand. Once in Kalka we changed for the train to Delhi. A totally different trip. The heat of the plains, overcrowded carriages, people climbing in the windows from the roof while the train was moving, and hundreds of people wanting to try their English. "What is your name?" "Where do you come from?" "Sydney - you must know my brother…". And the eternal "Baksheesh?"

Delhi was 44°C when we arrived. We had decided to stay in the old part of Delhi and took a couple of small rooms in a noisy hotel. All the hotels were noisy. This was a noisy town. We travelled from the railway station on a bicycle rickshaw. It was a scary trip weaving in and out of the traffic on pot-holed roads. And it was crazy how quick one guy peddling two people and baggage could go. Pedro's ride was a little easier as he was solo. The hotels were mostly run by kids. I'm talking ten to twelve years old. This one wasn't any different. The family were in the back room or not too far away, but they never appeared. The kids knew all the tricks and you would have to bargain for the room price. Somehow we always came away feeling like we'd be scammed. They nodded no when they said yes, and yes when they said no, so we didn't know what was going on.

It was too hot to eat so we just sipped hot chai and bought local outfits - cheesecloth pants and over-shirts. We mailed the rest of our winter clothing home. Another big half-day at the post office. This time we had to endure snail pace Indian bureaucracy as well as double-the-size queues and twice the confusion. One thing you learn very quickly in India is that you have to assert yourself. No pussy footing around or you get walked over. You don't need to be an arsehole but you do need to be decisive and demonstrative. In a respectful way. There are no such things as queues and get ready for a fight if you try to start one.

DWELLER ON THE THRESHOLD

At the post office we got a message from Rod saying he was no longer coming to India. He had crashed his car and had to use his savings to fix the other guy's ride. He was also very nervous about us sending him anything ... no packages had arrived so far. Pedro was furious. His watch was gone. For the remainder of the trip Pedro referred to rip-off merchants as Kashmiri Jons.

The Indians would do anything to get US dollars, your passport or a partner to marry. Anything that would give them a chance to get out of India. We met two French guys who had sold their passports, reported them stolen and after a protracted four week wait had new ones from their consulate. What a drama to make about five hundred dollars each. After about a week, and numerous refusals to sell Olga, we caught a five hour tour bus to Agra to see the Taj Mahal and the Red Fort.

In spite of it being about 50°C, the Taj was awesome. There are few things in the world that are as impressive and still in perfect condition after three hundred and fifty-odd years of baking in the sun. Huge, symmetrical, white marble rising out of its red desert surrounds and siding the Yamuna River, open to whatever breeze and fabulously ornate. What a privilege to visit it.

Emperor Shah Jahan must have loved his wife very much to build such a fabulous mausoleum monument. It really is one of the seven wonders of the world. It took twenty years to complete and cost the modern day equivalent of one billion US dollars. He didn't spare a cent and even had real rubies, emeralds and twenty eight different types of semi-precious stones embedded in the marble. It didn't help him though. Despite plans to build an exact replica in black onyx for himself on the other side of the river, he died of a broken heart shortly after the Taj was completed.

BOM BOM

The return bus ride home was exhausting and emotional. As we approached Delhi we came across a family whose motor scooter had been hit by a car in a roundabout and they all looked dead. Two adults and two children. No helmets. Just rag-like bodies scattered across the road. As a motorcyclist, scenes like this make me really sad. I could only imagine how hectic it was riding through that Delhi traffic. You took your life into your hands as a pedestrian, never mind getting motorised with four people on the one machine and carving your way through the chaos.

The roads were full of everything. I recall marvelling at one intersection where there was a bicycle rider balancing a four-poster, Queen-size bed on his head and he was manoeuvring his way around cars, buses, trucks, taxis, motorbikes, other cyclists, pedestrians, kids playing, wandering cows and a policeman standing point with a big cane and smashing everyone within reach. In amongst all of this was a guy driving a horse and cart with a stick buried in the horse's arse. He just pushed the stick when he wanted to go faster.

Delhi is an incredible place. You can buy anything ... if you know where to look. We even found a refreshment shop selling twenty different flavours of bhung drink, which is made with buffalo milk and the leaves and seeds of the marijuana plant. Not that strong but a great little pick me up. Marijuana (ganga) grew wild beside the roadsides throughout the country. The holy men or sadhus who worshipped Shiva would pick the roadside plants to stoke their chillums. Once they had the chillum alight they would honour Shiva by calling out "Bom Shanka" or "Awake Shiva" to sanctify their effort. For thousands of years they had honoured Shiva by using smoko to help them ponder deep religious and philosophical thoughts.

Marijuana was outlawed in India in the 1970s following U.S. and international treaties. Despite it being a core part of their society, Indian authorities destroyed farms and arrested farmers. Whole layers of commerce were removed and many people starved. Today they turn a blind eye to its existence and many locals even grow a little to give to visiting sadhus as a puja (offering) to the gods. Middle class Indians look upon ganga smokers in the same way westerners look upon people who drink too much.

Large numbers of Indians smoked locally made cigarettes which were as rough as. You could buy one at a time which suited their budget. Tourist imported duty-free smokes were worth their weight in gold and there were plenty who would pay it, just for the status, and they wouldn't even smoke them. The poorer Indians smoked Beedis which are mini-cigarettes made from tobacco flake wrapped in leaf and tied with string. Lots of others got a buzz from chewing the Areca nut with Betel leaf and spitting the red residue into the street. Both are highly addictive.

The volume of red spittle colouring the gutters and streets is evidence of how many enjoyed the habit.

One of the best things about India is their gods. There is a god for every one and for every situation. Brahma is the Creator, representing the universe and all within it. Saraswati is his wife and the Goddess of Learning. Brahma's avatars included Vishnu who enlightened Order and Harmony, with his wife Lakshmi the Godess of Good Fortune. Shiva, is the Protector and his son Ganesh the elephant boy, is the Forgiver and God of Luck. Rama is the hero of the epic drama, the Ramayana. His warrior helper is Hanuman the Monkey King. And Krishna, is the Teacher of the sacred scriptures. There are many more deities personifying Brahma's sacred attributes, thus allowing all groups to worship regardless of status, location or history.

After about a week of amazing stimulation and with Ganesh by my side we started looking for a cheap flight to Kathmandu. Cheap flight offices were everywhere in those days. You could get a "Round the World" ticket with half a dozen stops on Thai or Singapore Airlines for about $US500. Most European travellers bought one-way tickets to Delhi or Bangkok and then got a cheap flight home. It was a big thing buying a ticket. Retailers would ring wholesalers. Wholesalers would ring airlines. Lots of calls to get the best price. You'd have to hand over your passport to have the tickets printed and then they would be delivered to the shopfront. That usually meant having to go back the next day to collect them and you hoped like anything that your passport was included. If you learn anything in India, it is patience. If you weren't patient then you'd go crackers.

I remember getting into a tuk tuk after one of these ticket episodes. It was driven by a one-eyed Sikh with a patch, he looked like a comic character in his turban. About fifty metres into the ride he turned around and said: "You want to buy hasheeeesh". We looked at each other, nodded and smiled. He then drove into a side street where he pulled over and with great precision parked beside a small tubular post sticking upright out of the ground. He quietly leaned out and took the cap off the top of the post and pulled out a stash of hash that he had hidden. Crazy that he kept his stuff in such a public place, but it was obviously safe and accessible.

The alternative to flying to Kathmandu was to get a train and a bus, but that was a two-day exercise … just to buy the tickets. Then there were the train and bus rides which took another two days.

Catching trains in India is hard work. Finding your carriage and your seat in the short time a train stops at your station, with thousands of people pushing and shoving is very challenging. We tried travelling third class but learned very quickly not to do that. There were people pushing their bags in and out of the carriage windows and climbing in after them and over anyone who was already seated. On one occasion there was a legless beggar swinging from carriage window to carriage window with one arm while putting his free one inside for baksheesh money. He must have worked his way from one end of the train to the other, all while the train was travelling along.

The plane ride to Kathmandu was in a very old Air India DC3. It was the first time I'd flown. Very exciting. The roar and wind of the twin propellor motors, the build up of speed and the G-forces from the lift off. Unlike today you knew you were in the belly of a giant machine. Then the slow climb from the plains of India, up and over the foothills, and then up and over the mountains. It was so exciting peering out of the small porthole window and seeing the mountain spine running off into oblivion. It was a relatively quick flight and, before we knew it, we were landing in the cool, green Kathmandu Valley where a taxi ferried us under the city gateway sign "Kathmandu Top of the World", and into the medieval town centre.

We couldn't believe the amazingly ornate wood carved buildings, silhouetted by the snow-capped mountain ranges. There were hundreds of stone and timber shrines and every Hindu god was represented. The street markets and small shopfronts sold everything you could possibly imagine. Among the "modern" shops were the timeless cobblers, wood carvers, carpet weavers and wool spinners. Life was on display everywhere you looked.

DWELLER ON THE THRESHOLD

Tourism in Nepal was split between the hippies and the hikers. Two trekking companies seemed to control everything the hikers would need … and it wasn't cheap. The hikers would arrive from Europe or the States and stay in lodge-style hotel accommodation. They were kitted out and taken trekking. Everything was arranged so they didn't really get involved in the other aspects of the town. The hippies on the other hand wore the local clothes, ate in local restaurants and interacted with the local people.

The Nepalese people were great. A mixture of Hindus and Tibetans who were extremely warm, light-hearted, positive and tolerant. You felt safe as they had been looking after the hikers and hippies for years … not to mention the British and Allies in multiple world wars.

We took a couple of rooms above a restaurant on Freak Street. It was cheap and comfortable. The restaurant served western meals which were often finished off with a quiet hash joint and a coffee. You could even order a "special" mushroom omelette - which we avoided. We hadn't really taken to omelettes since our episode in Kabul, and the idea of going psycho in a strange town wasn't really smart, as the hippies would certainly take advantage of you.

The next day we saw a poster depicting Shiva smoking a chillum and it gave notice of the fine merchandise that was available from the Eden Hashish Centre, the location of which turned out to be just a few doors down from our hotel on Freak Street. There was all kinds of hashish, ganga and pipes. Some of the hash was brought in and sold on by the hippies. So there was smoko from Afghanistan, Pakistan, Kashmir and the foothills of Northern India, as well as the local selections. We hadn't tried the Nepalese hash before so we bought a few tolas to test it out and weren't disappointed.

We did lots of exploring through the narrow streets and made a few friends including Raj, a Nepalese boy who ran a handicrafts shop. I bought a few wooden and plastercast masks, some Tibetan Circle of Life Thangkas and rice paper paintings, and got him to ship them home for me.

By this time Pedro's funds were getting really low, so he figured he'd leave Nepal ASAP and head to Bangkok where he would suss out a cheap flight home. We agreed to meet him there in a few weeks. It was sad to see Pedro go, as he'd been my wing-man for so long, and we'd been through so much together. Despite all, he still had a great sense of humour and laughed about meeting us with a bride in Bangkok. I felt concerned by the bride comment, but happy that I'd see him again for one last holiday hoorah.

Olga and I then met a Dutch couple who had cycled a lot in Europe. They were about five years older than us and their names were Mila and Max. They were skinny from travelling in India and Mila's hair was henna red, green, yellow and blue. She looked like an Australian rosella parrot. Max's arms and legs were covered in tattoos, including a ying yang, an Om sign and some great Indian deities that he had inked in Bombay. They managed to convince us to rent bikes and ride from Kathmandu to Pokhara, 160 kilometres away in the north-west, at the foothills of the Annapurna mountains.

We left at about eight am and climbed our way out of the valley, up, up and up until we reached the ridge at about lunchtime. The road ahead zig-zagged down into the next valley. It was tarred for one car and had dirt surrounds that fell away on one side to the next level down. You'd be dead if you slipped up, but there was no traffic so we rode the centre line. My off-road experience came in handy and I kept a watchful eye on Olga who pottered along behind us.

The journey to the river below took about two hours. I hadn't concentrated like that for a long time. What a ride! I didn't peddle once. Lining up corner after corner. Trying to miss the potholes and gravel. I stopped a few times to wait for Olga to catch up and we took time out at the bottom to recover. There was a beautiful grassy riverside area so we had a swim, and lay around sharing chillums, nuts and chocolate. The Dutchies then pulled out pocket pistols they had bought in Pakistan for about $25 a piece. They were single-shot close-range Derringers. We had some fun using up their ammo before they tossed the guns into the river. Gone! They figured they were heading into more civilised and policed countries and no longer needed the protection. Travelling from Pakistan to Nepal they had only needed to show the guns once. Funnily, they scattered a small mob of Pakistanis that were hassling Mila in Lahore.

We then rode along the valley floor for a few hours and found a small school house where we bunked down for the night. The caretakers were great. I don't think a lot of tourists ever stopped midway to Pokhara. Our hosts moved out after cooking us a dahl and rice dinner. They slept close by in the stables.

The next morning we pushed on, occasionally waving to the passing tourist mini buses, and late that day made it in to Pokhara. We were exhausted … but what a beautiful place. What a beautiful ride to get there. Pokhara was a small town by Lake Phewa Tal at the foothills of the Himalayas. The lake had lots of little islands and each hosted a Lingam shrine to Shiva. I got a great photo of Olga crouched over an erect one and releasing her "Kundalini" energy.

There was a small airport nearby that brought the trekkers in. It was just an open field where they had to chase the cattle off the runway every time a plane circled for landing.

At the Rainbow Hotel we met a wild Italian guy who looked like a local hills-man. It turned out he had been high up in the mountains and winter had closed in. He tried to walk down but it was hard going through the blinding snow and wind. He was dying of cold when a little Himalayan holy man found him and took him back to his cave where he spent the next 4 months until the weather came good. He was a real trip. I think the excitement of speaking to other westerners, even in broken English, was more than he could take. We stayed for a few days, soaking up sun and the view and smoking chillums with the Italian guy, before packing the bikes on to the roof of a mini-bus for the return trip to Kathmandu.

We had left some of our gear at our Kathmandu hotel and the manager had moved it into their rooftop room where we stayed for another week. It was great as we had the whole roof to ourselves. We would sit up there drinking chai, smoking chillums, reading, meditating and watching the sunset and moon risings. It was a beautiful time and Olga and I had some real quality time together.

One day we took a flight in a small single engined plane along the Himalayas to see Everest up close. It was totally mad given that Sir Edmund Hillary's wife and daughter had crashed and died in a similar plane a few months earlier. What an amazing view travelling so close to the range and then seeing that awe-inspiring pyramid called Everest. It really provided perspective to the whole trekking thing.

The time had come to say goodbye to Middle Asia and travel down into South East Asia. We were sad as we knew we were leaving one world for another. And Kathmandu was a very special place, unique in time. We vowed to come back and wondered if we ever would.

We had explored going overland to Bangkok but getting to Bangladesh and through jungle Burma and Thailand was impossible so we bought a cheap flight on Thai Airways direct to Bangkok. This flight was a big step up from our DC3 out of Delhi. It was a proper plane with meals and air conditioning – what a treat.

We arrived at Kathmandu airport still holding a tola of hash. We just never got around to smoking it. We couldn't throw it away so we divided it up. Half was taped to the underside of my toes and since I was wearing thongs, I figured no one was going to suspect. We ate the rest and it took forever to take effect. In fact, the flight was just levelling out from take-off when I got the rush. It was an explosion in my head and I felt sick. I was in a cold sweat.

We were sitting outside the curtain that separated economy from business class. I could see the toilet door behind the curtain and without saying anything made a lunge for it. On my way through I was intercepted by a hostess who blocked my way. Thankfully there was an empty seat, so I crash landed in it and passed out. When I woke I found two or three crew standing over me trying to collect some information about my malaise. I felt a lot better after sleeping it off and blamed the episode on the mango chutney curry that I had eaten at the airport. Perfectly feasible. The hostie then opened the curtain to economy where Olga was still seated. Olga was off her tree and really worried. She had sensed the commotion on the other side of the curtain but was too out of it to step through to see what was going on.

Getting through customs was easy enough in Bangkok. Out on the street it was crazy busy and sticky hot. I had not experienced that intensity of human life and noise before. Yes, I had been to India but this was a frenetic step beyond that. Everything happened at twice the speed. Our taxi into town was no different. It raced along the outside lane. Up ahead there was a car stopped in our lane. It must have broken down and it was just sitting there. We thought our driver had seen it, so we watched on. The car was looming fast and I yelled, waking the driver who swerved and almost lost the cab in a roll over. In the smoke of burning rubber we lurched to a stop and looked back to see the car that almost killed us. The driver was super apologetic and we knew he meant it, as his normally brown face was about as white as ours. A close call!

It was then an unnecessarily slow trip, as the driver cautiously drove the rest of the way to our recommended cheap accommodation on Sukkamvit Road. We entered through a bustling, flaming noodle restaurant, then up a big stairway to the rooms which, as it turned out, were well-used brothel cubicles. Lots of doorways with a stream of people going in and out.

We sat down on our bed, leaned across and locked the door, and tried to move around our gear. What the hell we were doing there? I know we were consciously trying to minimise our spend as our funds were getting low, but this was cheap. Real cheap! You could hear all sorts of things through the walls so we thought it best to get out and have a wander around.

Coming in from the airport the cabbie told stories of cops busting travellers in their hotel rooms. I figured they would never find us at this hotel but I got paranoid and untaped the small piece of hash on my foot. We ate most of it and threw the last bit into a spittoon as we were heading out into the street.

The traffic was ridiculous. So many bikes, cars and trucks, all going way too fast between traffic lights. There must have been eight lanes in each direction. We set off to look for Pedro. We had no idea where he was but thought we'd check the European hotels. There were a lot of them and they were spread across the city. It was stinking hot and humid but we finally found him quietly reading in an air conditioned hotel foyer. He was very glad to see us. He had his ticket home and his money had all but run out. I was glad there was no bride bedside him and told him so. The next day he was leaving to go back to Sydney. We had one last meal together and reflected on our adventure.

It was sad but we were excited for Pedro as he had been stretching his money for quite a while and now he was going home after just over a year on the road. He was a lot skinnier, his hair was longer and he was definitely wiser for the experience. We reflected on our trip through Europe, the tea bags that saved our lives, Ryan's ability to sniff out the acid on Mykonos and in Athens, his getting busted in Afghanistan, the omelette in Kabul, our time in the "riverside" hotel in Mingora, the Rasool Jon rip-off in Srinagar, and the crazy bus rides and times in India. There was lots of Pedro's loud laughing and the vibe was really good. Pedro was my blood brother and Olga was his sister. In the end we gave him a giant hug and watched him disappear into the hotel lift.

Olga and I still had some money and we intended hanging out for as long as we could. We had no real plan but had each other and held hands and walked slowly back to the hotel. While in a reflective mood we wondered what Troy and Ryan were up to and thought they'd missed the best part of the journey by not travelling to India.

Bangkok was full of Europeans, it was a long way from their home but it was probably the first access point they had to South

East Asia. In the hotel lobbies there was even more chat about cops raiding the hotels looking for drugs. There was a lot of heroin and opium about as well as Thai sticks or Buddha sticks as many people called them. Buddha sticks were basically the marijuana heads taken off their stalks and wrapped with a hair of hemp twine around a pencil-sized bamboo sliver. You just unwrapped what you wanted to smoke. Very potent.

Bangkok has amazing Buddhist temples, great street food and thousands of fried noodle restaurants. On one trip we found a giant open-air restaurant the size of a footy oval which was really good value. Mostly seafood. To enter you walked through a big-top style tent, found the fish you liked swimming about in a tank, and placed your order. Somehow that fish got cooked and delivered to your table. We were amazed they remembered what the fish and you looked like, and how they found where you were sitting in the crowd.

Sex was a big industry in Bangkok. There were clubs, bars and brothels packed into the red light areas, and they had spilt out into every crevice and corner of the city. You couldn't go anywhere without being accosted by girls or lady-boys. They worked in groups and like a cattle round-up they could cut a guy out from his group, march him off to a convenient room and smother him with body parts while they ransacked his clothing. Even the most prudish guys would be crazy to carry anything except a few dollars and their hotel key.

One of the great things about Bangkok was the air-conditioned shopping malls. After being in India where there was never any relief, it was fantastic to cool off while wandering around the silks, tourist handicrafts and airline shops. We did a quick pass through the main post office to the Poste Restante section to see if anyone had left us mail or messages. There was mail from home and a message from Pedro telling us where he was staying. That would have made finding him easier but it was a bit late now. He was gone and I was going to miss him.

There wasn't a lot to report from friends back home so we counted our blessings and started to plan the next leg of our trip. Up until then we hadn't really given this a lot of thought as we were focussed on getting to Bangkok. We had a bit over $US1000 between us. Not enough to do anything long term but enough to travel overland down through Malaysia to Indonesia and island hop our way to Timor and Darwin. Probably the sensible choice at this point.

Olga told me of twin friends from New York who had worked in Japan as strippers and made a small fortune. I also recalled some people whom we had met who had taught English there and had enjoyed similar rewards. I wasn't really into Japan, as it was really flimsy information, and a big step to go to such an intensely straight society after where we had been.

Meanwhile the rainy season had set in and many parts of Bangkok were flooded. We invested in new thongs (flip flops as Olga called them) with a really thick sole to keep you out of the damp. We then rolled up our pants and walked miles every day to take in the sights. We avoided entering the tourist temples and attractions, which meant we saw a lot of the city that tourists wouldn't normally get to. The Chinese quarter was interesting and largely untouched by foreigners.

A lot of travellers were going up north to Chang Mai to get out of the wet so we decided to postpone the big decisions and try to travel that bit further into Laos. It took a few days to get a Lao visa and then we were on the long bus ride north. We passed through farms cut into jungle countryside until late afternoon when we arrived in Udon Thani in northern Thailand. We were just in time to take a boat across the Mekong River and to catch a cab into Vientiane, the capital of Laos.

Vientiane was a relatively small city and a former French colony so the architecture was a beautiful mix of French colonial and Buddhist temples. The civil war (US backed anti-communist forces against the People's Army of Vietnam, the Pathet Lao) was coming to an end. The Pathet Lao were in control but the CIA were still in town. There was a strange feeling on the streets which was articulated by our taxi driver when he observed: "You can't break the law in Vientiane - everything is legal".

The driver took us to the Hotel Constellation which had been used by foreign correspondents and journalists during the Vietnam war. It was a classic French Colonial building with balconies over the street.

After breakfast the next day we ventured out to get a feeling for the town. Across the road was a hut that sold grocery-style items and next door to that was an opium den. It didn't have a sign. You could just tell by the smell. I thought it was a strange place to have an opium den but Olga suggested it was probably well-frequented by the journos during the war. The owner was a very skinny, very old, Laotian man with grey hair, a long beard and faraway eyes. He sat cat-like sunning himself on a rope bed out front. With time to kill we asked if we could enter. He waved us in.

Inside, the cat came to life in the dark. He was agile and aware and escorted us to a grass mat where we lay until he came around with a very ornate Chinese-style pipe with silver engravings of fire-breathing dragons. Very appropriate. He tore off a small piece of opium from a ball he had in his pocket and stuck a thin bamboo stick into it and held it over an oil lamp until it started smouldering. Then away we went. The feeling was familiar - cloudy mind, warm body and nauseous tummy. This settled as we drifted into a dreamy interlude. The old cat busied himself making green tea which he offered in bamboo cups. It was bitter but refreshing. After a few hours we started to come around and left to wander the streets. What a way to start the day! The sun was shining. It was cool and there wasn't a lot of foot or car traffic. The town was surprising clean and slow compared to Bangkok.

Because of the war the exchange rate was ridiculously low. Instead of getting about seventy Kip to the dollar we were getting seven thousand! They wanted US dollars badly. We thought we should go down to the jewellery shop to buy gold. They weren't that stupid. Gold was priced in US dollars. But we did get amazing value from everywhere else as the locals still accepted the Kip. We ate great French cuisine and drank French wine at high class restaurants at night and probably had the cheapest stay anywhere on our trip.

There was a giant undercover market in the town centre. It sold everything you could imagine. The tobacco stall was huge like one of the country-region displays at the Royal Easter Show. It had a great selection of tobacco leaf, cigarettes, kif, ganga, opium and giant Buddha sticks. We bought two foot-long sticks to have during our stay. We didn't have to go back to the opium den again as the sticks were obviously grown in the fields with the poppies and were wickedly strong. We only used small bits in a pipe and with just one or two puffs we were gone. I think we threw one of the sticks away when it was time to leave.

During our week-long stay we contemplated going up into the hills to visit the Mnong tribes but were warned off this as fighting was still underway with the Pathet Lao forces chasing down the last of the opposition. The real tragedy to this fight was that the local hills-men, who had sided with the US, were now being wiped out.

Our trip back to Bangkok was a bit of a daze as we had a final puff of our Buddha before we bordered the bus. That evening we tried a different budget hotel. A bit more touristy. The rooms were larger and cleaner and we were on the sixth floor with a small window with a view over the city. You really got another perspective on the number of waterways interconnecting things when you got up high. Our floor was still very busy, as there were lots of locals and junkies wandering the corridors and yelling and screaming so we turned up the noisy aircon to drown out the buzz. After about thirty minutes of its tractor-like rumble and no relief from the heat, we shut it down and tried to sleep off the big trip back.

The next day was decision day so out came the tarot cards. We sat on the bed and asked two questions: Do we travel to Japan? Do we travel to Australia? One reading was resoundingly positive and the other was negative. We now had a clearer picture of where we were heading next. Surprisingly it was Japan. The cards said we would have positive results in love and business and would meet people who would support us. We had no idea of the detail but figured we'd get there and try and get some work teaching English and, if we ran out of cash, we could always head home.

We managed to get a really good deal on the airline tickets. One way Bangkok to Tokyo with a stop over in Hong Kong. Over the next few days we did one more round of the city and headed to the airport. The flight was uncomplicated but the landing in Hong Kong was unnerving with the plane navigating its way through a corridor of buildings on both sides of its landing approach. You could see into the apartment windows as you flew by. It was a trip you definitely wouldn't want to take with a crosswind.

DWELLER ON THE THRESHOLD

...it took a few days to get a Lao visa... and then we were on the long bus ride north to Udon Thani... We were just in time to get a boat across the Mekong and bus to Vientiane...

Hong Kong was vastly different from our previous destinations. There were a lot of rich Chinese, cashed up holiday-makers from Europe and Australia, and plenty of ritzy hotels and shops. Finding a budget hotel was a challenge but we found somewhere reasonable in an old apartment block on Nathan Road. That night we took the ferry across to the island and headed for the Tiger Balm Gardens at the top of the lookout.

Looking down from the lookout was mind blowing. We could see all the tall apartment buildings stacked on top of one another. It was crazy how big and close they were to each other. It was also scary being up there by ourselves. I revisited all the kung fu movies I had seen to be ready for any engagement. Thank god nothing happened as we had our passports and what little cash on us.

The next morning we started planning our journey to Japan. We realised we had nothing civilised to wear so we went downtown to get some smart clothes made up. I chose a light green fabric and was measured for a casual suit. Olga went with a blue silk skirt and jacket. Even though we were short on money it seemed like a good investment. Mind you looking back on my green suit, I'm not sure what I was thinking. We covered a fair bit of the town and while exploring I found an interesting Chinese antiques shop where I scored a great set of three very old i-Ching coins. That afternoon a typhoon blew up and ripped through the city. The rain thrashed down, everything rattled and flooded and it was dangerous on the street. We bunkered in our room and watched out our window as everything that was not nailed down flew past. It was scary so we put the mattress up against the window and spent the night trying to sleep. The next morning the typhoon was gone but it was a mess and very wet on the street. The thick flip flops from Bangkok came into their own again.

We had to wait a few days before the tailors finished our clothes so I thought I would go to the hospital, to see if they could give me something for my Nepalese stomach. It had been playing up for about a month and I was over it. The hospital passed me on to the Infectious Diseases Unit and before I knew it I was in a hospital bed so they could do some testing. I had to stay overnight. The results came back the next morning and they had no idea what the problem was, so I checked myself out. It was a long walk back to the hotel … about three hours in the muggy heat.

Olga wasn't around when I got there and when she did return she was smacked out. Apparently she met a German guy who was holding and they got high together. I was pretty upset as we had agreed that there would be no heroin and definitely no shooting up. The idea of becoming a junkie or getting hepatitis in this part of the world was a death sentence.

After a few tense days we went back to the tailor for the final fitting and a cheap pair of shoes. We looked pretty sharp, in fact good enough to hit the casino in Macau. Olga was going to clean up on the blackjack table. Blackjack was supposedly her card thing after the Tarot.

Macau was a quick hydrofoil ride south and a chance to see the Territories from the water. We had twenty dollars set aside to gamble and not surprisingly Olga was soon out of money. Still, it was my first casino experience and a good night out. The next day we boarded a JAL flight to Tokyo. The Japanese hosties were fabulous with their orchestrated safety routine. Lots of gentle arm waving which reminded me of a Tai Chi class. All highly civilised except for the number of people who smoked cigarettes and the stink it left in the cabin.

CHAPTER FIVE

In Walked Luck

We had heard that the Immigration guys in Japan were pretty tough, so we wore our suits. Our hair was as tidy as we could get it. The only telltale sign was the luggage. My backpack and Olga's duffle bag were pretty scruffy. On the declaration card we confirmed we had $US200 in cash and that we had Travellers Cheques for another thousand. The Travellers Cheques were bullshit and we hoped like hell they wouldn't ask to look at them. Thankfully they didn't ask and generously gave us a three month visa. It was amazing what a suit could do.

Tokyo was a vast city and amazingly clean. We didn't know where to go but had seen a notice board at the airport for a "traveller's rate" tatami hotel in the centre of town - so we headed there.

The grass mat and paper-walled room was about fifty dollars a night so we bunkered down to sleep off the big day of travelling.

Lying there we realised we were in a dire situation and would only have a few days to get a job or a flight home. We didn't talk about which home we would go to but I think mine was the closest and had the best support network. The big problem was we didn't have the money to pay for the flight. How we were going to get around that was still to be discussed.

Next morning we ventured out. There was a coffee shop down the street where a few traveller types were hanging out. Coffee breakfast for two cost us $US60. Shit! We started to get really scared. We didn't know anyone, we didn't speak the language and there weren't a lot of options. The tarot had dropped us right in the middle of one of the most expensive cities in the world. The hand of fate was on us now. We headed off to the YMCA to compare room rates and see if anyone had any ideas on where we could get work.

As we stepped out into the street we met a Japanese guy with an American accent. He asked if we would you like to make $200 a day each. Without hesitation, and in sync, we said "Yes". It felt suspect as it was a lot of money but we accepted his card with a responsive bow.

He explained he was looking for European dancers to work in clubs and that it was easy work. I could see Olga's brain turning over. I asked him what the chances were of teaching English, and he said that it wasn't that easy, as you needed to belong to an agency, have qualifications, and it took time to set up. I was dejected and didn't know what to say next. The guy seemed affable enough so we said we'd think about it and went to sit and reflect.

After a few hours of looking long and hard at his card we realised we had no choice. We had heard of clubs that employed western girls to act as hosts and ply customers with drinks. We kind of hoped this was the case and that it was a progressive club that also hired guys.

We didn't have a phone to call this Larry guy, so we got a city map and worked out from his business card where he located. Shortly after we were on a train across the city. We followed the map until there wasn't any further detail. A policeman was in the general vicinity so we asked directions, there was a language barrier, so we showed him Larry's card and he pointed out the apartment block. Next thing we were ringing the doorbell. A surprised Larry answered and couldn't believe his eyes. There we were in front of him. We recounted our journey and the policeman's help to which he quickly looked around and shut the door behind us.

Larry made a pot of green tea and we asked lots of questions. It then became obvious he wasn't looking for hosts or even girls to dance. He was looking for couples to dance. I started to get pretty anxious. Larry said there were Super Strip clubs all over Japan where dancers performed sexy moves on stage to audiences of businessmen. He explained that dancers were employed for a ten-day stint and then moved on to a different club … or you could drop out. He was an agent who had a troop of dancers, mostly westerners. He was happy to pay $US200 in cash every day, to each of us. It didn't take a genius to work out we could make four grand for ten days work and we would have enough to get back on the hippie trail, where this money could last another six months.

With a sense of despair and appreciation we agreed. The next change over for the dancers was in two days time in Yokohama. He encouraged us to get some music, buy a costume and work up an act. Larry had a lot of music so Olga sat down to put four tracks together. We had ten minutes of dancing to fill, and before long Larry was dubbing off a cassette for us to take away. Larry then asked what sort of moves we envisaged so we set about creating a dance sequence. It was very naive and must have been funny because Larry was laughing a lot.

He then asked what stage name we would like to use so he could inform the venue managers. We decided on Peter & Olga, a salute to Pedro, and we made arrangements to meet on Sunday morning at Tokyo railway station for the trip to Yokohama. Larry would come with us.

We left his apartment with a one hundred dollar yen advance and headed to a Ginza department store to buy a costume. Olga came away with a sparkly top and matching briefs and, with little choice, I bought a pair of plain black briefs.

Back at our hotel we couldn't believe what just happened. I flashed on some lyrics from David Bowie's *Golden Years* and turned to Olga and sang *"In walked luck and you looked in time, never look back, walk tall, act fine"*. She gave me a hug as if to say: *"I'll stick with you, baby, for a thousand years"*. We endlessly refined our dance. Olga shaved her legs and underarms and we hacked back our small jungles. We then gave each other haircuts and asked the managers if we could leave our luggage in the back room to collect in the future.

Sunday came around quickly. Next thing we were on the bullet train to Yokohama with an overnight bag and not a lot in it. The train was very impressive and so was Mount Fuji zipping past. We both must have been super nervous as we started to itch and, after slowing our breathing, we put the itching down to the hair trimming.

The venue was low key. It was just a shop front in a suburb. Once inside it was a small theatre with a stage and space for an audience of about one hundred people. We went around the back and were introduced to the manager who showed us the facilities. There was a large makeup room in traditional tatami style with about a dozen Japanese girls in various states of undress. The manager spoke to them and I heard the words "Peter and Olga san". The other performers bowed a hello. The manager then showed us another tatami room where we could sleep and the bathing area. Then Larry was off.

We were on our own. The girls were friendly and inquisitive and there were many introductions. I didn't remember any of them as my head was in another place. The first show was coming up at one pm and we were scheduled last on the roster. We figured it was a good chance to check out the other acts to see how ours compared. We took a place at the back of what was a half-full house of plastic-shoed businessmen, and watched as each girl danced, stripped, and in the final music piece flung her legs open for audience inspection. They called the leg opener "Hai Dozo", which translated as "Yes Please". Olga and I looked at each other and realised our routine was a long way short of expectation.

The nerves were setting in big time and the acts were turning over at a great rate. Soon it was our turn to get "dressed" and with the familiar blaring beat of the first song, Olga leapt out on stage to what was now a packed audience of very quiet men. She danced and wiggled a lot and then it was my turn to march in with the second track. I puffed up and stood there in some sort of macho stance while she danced around trying to get my attention. She then rubbed herself all over me, throwing her top off and then crouching down in front and simulating oral sex …

as planned the audience couldn't see anything. She then removed her briefs and pushed me to the ground, she climbed on top, pretended to mount me and started grinding and flailing about. We pretended to be climaxing, and on cue Olga squealed with the music and then the scene was over. I rolled over and moved off stage while she moved around the stage edge showing her bits in "Hai Dozo" to all that wanted to see. There was a crowd as the chance to see a foreign girl was an obvious treat. The music ended, there was no clapping and the lights went up. It was over. My god what an experience. It was such a daggy act, they didn't clap, we were so embarrassed.

Olga and I went backstage, and the girls who had all been watching, politely nodded while we shrank into a corner. It was then we came to the realisation that we would have to do this three more times that day and for the next nine days.

The manager came in to see us and in his broken English, and with an index finger pointing and poking into circled fingers, he tried to explain how we might improve. It was obviously not what they had expected or were paying for. The manager felt he wasn't getting through so he took us into his office and rang Larry. I think Larry was expecting the call. He knew that they didn't want simulated sexy dancing. They wanted the real thing. He said we should try to offer more sexy moves and that it would be worthwhile to us if we wanted continued employment.

Back in our room we went through an array of emotions. In reality it was me going through the emotions as Olga had already shown her bits and was accepting of the situation. What could we do, but submit. The next show was coming up so we devised a way of spicing it up. Then there was that music again, we were off, it was a full house. Out on stage I felt like deer in headlights

IN WALKED LUCK

but tried to switch off and focus on Olga. This time there was no simulation and I had no trouble rising to the occasion and leaving Olga to show a very wet pussy to her admiring crowd.

We came off stage laughing nervously at the absurdity of it all and there was the manager shaking my hand. By this time, I was shaking all over so Olga hugged me quietly and said if this is what they wanted then we would give it to them. Doing the job was easy enough, but doing it in front of everyone was a real head trip. The third and fourth shows went by in similar fashion and somehow I was ready for each. It was really difficult when you thought about it, but we refined the act each time. It turned out that the Japanese liked my portrayal of a macho guy and Olga going after it, so I played it up. They also liked that they could see it all, and they loved Olga's body. It was unlike any of the Japanese girls and possibly the first time they had seen a gaijin up close. And the fact they didn't clap was no reflection of how much they enjoyed themselves. The venue manager explained that Japanese men are very quiet.

At the end of the night the manager came around with envelopes for each of the performers. We thanked him and bowed. After he left we opened the envelope to find a wad of thousand yen notes that added up to four hundred dollars. I shook Olga's hand and we hugged with a sigh of relief. This happened every night except Saturday when we were expected to do six shows (Larry didn't mention this), but in recognition of the extra "work" we got two envelopes. The second had another two hundred dollars worth of yen.

The drama of the first day had passed and we did the best we could to deliver a great act. Thankfully I was twenty-one and had no trouble meeting the demands of four to six shows a day and often had intimate moments with Olga at night after it was all over.

Strangely the audience really helped us deal with the whole thing as they didn't yell out or cheer or clap. The lights were very bright so it was hard to see what the audience were getting up to but I think it was pretty tame. The important thing was they didn't judge so we only had ourselves to deal with. The other girls warmed up a lot.

IN WALKED LUCK

After a few days in Yokohama the itch that we had first felt on the train got to a point where, on closer inspection, we realised it was crabs. Probably from that hotel room in Hong Kong. We managed to buy a bottle of methylated spirits and doused our crotches. It burnt like hell, but we scrubbed, washed and then jumped into the hot tub only to leave an oily film and a few hundred dead bugs. I tried to change the water in the tub but couldn't figure it out. Embarrassingly, I had to leave it. The theatre managers didn't say anything but replaced the water the next morning.

We spent our days reading and, when we could, exploring the town. We couldn't really go far, as the first show was at lunchtime and someone had taken a liking to my Thai flip flops so I had no shoes. The cheap ones from Hong Kong were in my backpack. I was stuck wearing slippers.

The girls we were sharing with were lovely people. They were keen to share food and makeup ideas with Olga. They also loved her wild, wavy hair and would often brush it. I got used to sharing with naked girls and tried not to look when they were pruning for "Hai Dozo". One day a masseuse came in and one-by-one gave each of us a shiatsu (pressure point) massage. What a great treat ... and it was on the house.

The money came every night and was starting to add up but there was nowhere we could put it. It ended up in the overnight bag. We started to worry about it but soon realised that the Japanese were so respectful of one's personal space and property that any paranoia quickly disappeared.

At about day six Larry rang to say he had a booking for us in Sapporo. It was a city on the north island. He wanted to know if were on board and we figured we'd take the money for as long as we could get it. Early on the eleventh day the theatre manager put us on a plane and at the other end a mini-bus picked us up to take us to the venue. It was only a short drive into town, but the bus drove very slowly while the driver spoke on a loudspeaker attached to the roof. Every now and then we would recognise our names "Peter and Olga san". He eventually stopped and parked in the nightclub precinct.

We got out and had a good look around. It was late morning but there were already bright show lights and a lot of people about. The bus was covered in writing and had a sign on the roof. I asked our contact what the signage said and he explained it introduced Peter and Olga Live at the Super Strip club. We couldn't believe it. So upfront. We really didn't know how legal the whole thing was but we figured it must have been accepted as it was so public.

The nightclub was on steroids compared to the sleepy place in Yokohama. It had disco lights. There were pictures of some of the famous acts on the wall by the stairway and there was a much bigger bar and stage. The music was already blaring. The backstage area was tiny so they put us up in a tatami hotel down the street.

Our act was getting stronger and we weren't leaving anything to anyone's imagination. It was kind of fun once we had relaxed into what we were doing. There were three other foreign girls at this venue. They were professional strippers from Venezuela and were voluptuous beauties and outrageous Latinos. Loud and upfront. We had some great drinking sessions after work and they were stoked to find people who spoke English and Spanish (Olga). The girls hadn't had a couple-act like ours on their roster before and thought I was a superman. They had been in Japan a while and were horny as, and they wanted a piece of the action, including Olga. Not something one would normally refuse, but Olga and I were both afraid of being eaten alive by these three and we made up lots of excuses not to party on.

Essentially there were about a dozen performers at each venue. Most were Japanese but there were a number of internationals on the circuit. Some of the Japanese girls started out in full kimonos and danced to traditional music. Some were dressed as schoolgirls, some as office workers, and some were lesbian lovers. Most of the time they were demure and climaxed with a whimper. In contrast the western girls were loud and squealed with much delight. The girls from Venezuela were over the top, doing Mardi Gras, and shaking their big boobies and rousing the normally quiet audience into arm waving and a rapturous clap at the end of their performance.

Sapporo was a great town with lots of underground shopping arcades that must have been a godsend when the winter snows hit. I finally got to buy a pair of shoes, and I also bought a pair of Canadian hiking boots for a planned trek in Nepal once all of this was over. I also found and bought a really good book on the i-Ching and studied it in great detail. Unfortunately the i-Ching coins I had bought in Hong Kong were in my stored backpack so I mocked up some local coins and practiced a lot with them.

The i-Ching was devised about two and a half thousand years ago and even used by Confucius as a guide to making moral decisions. Throwing the three coins six times allowed you to build a hexagram of yin (value 2) and yang (value 3) lines. There are sixty-four hexagrams in the i-Ching with commentaries on each. These commentaries had been refined by philosophers over the years and, despite numerous historical Chinese book burnings, the i-Ching had survived.

Our ten show days zipped by and our next stop was a small club in the Ginza in Tokyo. We had to play it a bit more low key there as the owners didn't want to draw too much attention from the police. It became very obvious our act wasn't legal and we were more than happy that there were a few bouncers hanging around. They were all big, black-suited boys and all wore diamond rings on their pinky fingers. I figured they were Yakuza, which was Japanese Mafia. One day one of them stripped down to show off his tattoo. It was a full body piece with just his hands, feet and neck clean. And it was the most amazing coloured artwork depicting the Japanese flower card designs made famous in the late 1800s by Nintendo, who we know went on to video game fame.

We met a girl on this stint who was a French traveller. Her name was Cookie and she kept complaining that her boyfriend was dating Japanese girls while she was working. She wanted him involved in a couples act like ours. Cookie was a petite and fine featured twenty-eight-year-old, with a dark tan, long black hair and great silver jewellery. When she wasn't in her birthday suit she dressed in long flowery dresses, ballet shoes and silk tops. She was a real pixie.

One night after work, we went clubbing and met her guy. His name was Hugo. He was a few years younger than Cookie, medium height, skinny, shoulder length wavy black hair and didn't look like he'd seen the sun for quite a while. He was French/Italian and his life was on a high. He was having fun partying, so I jokingly said he should stop spending money and partner up with Cookie to make some. Cookie was right onto it but he was unconvinced. He did come to see the show the next day and the feedback was he needed more time to think about it.

IN WALKED LUCK

As it turned out Cookie and Hugo had been to Australia earlier on their trip. It was Christmas 1974. They were travelling in Asia and had secured their Aussie visas in Singapore. From there they took a boat down to Timor. It was the monsoon season so they were keen to keep moving and managed to get a small Fokker to fly them on to Darwin. There was a short stopover in Kupang where the sky darkened and the rains came on strong. They were lucky to take off as the runway was flooded and the plane slid as it built up speed. With their hearts in their mouths they crossed the Timor Sea and eventually landed in Darwin. Luckily, they passed unchallenged through customs, and once settled were able to enjoy some grass they had hidden in their undies.

Darwin was a long way from Ibiza, Phuket and Kuta which were the European hot spots of the day. It was a barren place, only made interesting by its Aboriginal, Islander, European and Asian cultural mix. The travellers there were mostly English on their way to or from Asia.

Hugo and Cookie stayed in a share-house with some people who knew some people. They had about two hundred dollars between them so Hugo got a cleaning job while Cookie tried to set up a traveller's cheque scam. Cookie was pretty hard core and had been in trouble with the law back in France. If there was a scam she knew about it. She had bought a stolen passport and travellers cheques from some other Frenchies in India and changed the photo in the passport to cash the cheques. She then bought legitimate cheques and sold those so she could claim they were stolen and have them replaced. I couldn't keep up.

With two weeks until Christmas the celebrations were well underway. There were parties everywhere. And there were lots of public announcements of an approaching cyclone. *"Please shut your windows. Stock up on food and water. Do not go out if the wind increases".* This went on for several days but miraculously the cyclone changed its mind and turned away. The warnings stopped. Danger was going somewhere else and life went on as normal.

Then, a few days before Christmas, the urgent warnings returned … and, of course, no one took any notice. The celebrations were in full swing. Parties everywhere. Nothing was going to stop the fun. On Christmas Eve, Cookie and Hugo went to a get together just few blocks away from where they were staying. The wind was up and it was raining.

The party was raging while the wind got wildly fast and scary. Then at two minutes to midnight there was a huge green flash in the sky and the power went out. Cyclone Tracy had hit! They shit themselves and ran to the bathroom where they got into the bathtub pulling all the towels they could find over themselves. Hugo said he repented that night and made peace with god as the walls and roof were ripped off the house.

Darwin was completely flattened, torn apart, seventy-one people died and there was half a billion dollars worth of damage. There was no help. When the rest of Australia woke up on Christmas Day the reality set in but it was days and weeks before heavy equipment arrived to search the rubble.

Cookie and Hugo had to leave the town. There was no food, water or shelter. They found a random car and with the couple whose house they were sharing, drove it over to North Queensland and down the coast to Sydney. It was a journey of about four and a half thousand kilometres. An amazing experience through an amazing landscape.

Australians unite in times of adversity and Cookie and Hugo, as registered victims of Tracy, received coupons from the government for fuel, meals and shelter. It was a real leg-up given they had arrived in and left Darwin with bugger all money.

For many months they lived in Sydney, working in restaurants and selling clothes at the markets so they could stash away money for a flight back to Asia. They eventually made their way to Bangkok where they met Larry who was there to drum up dancing talent for the Japan circuit. Cookie was immediately sold on the idea but Hugo didn't want to know. However he did agree to go with her and about two weeks later we were introduced to them in Tokyo.

Hugo had another great story for us. It happened on his first trip away from home. He had left Paris for Kabul as a pillion passenger on his mate's 1958 BSA. They got as far as Turkey before it blew up, so they abandoned it there and took buses the rest of the way. On board they made friends with two Italian guys and the four of them arrived unscathed in Herat where they met two Afghani tribesmen who agreed to sell them a kilo of hash each.

The boys followed the Afghanis to a house where they fired up a hubble bubble to test the quality. After numerous finger-sized pieces of beautiful black hash were smoked, they ended up absolutely legless. Hugo was lying on the floor half dazed and looked up at the bearded, turbaned Afghans. They were laughing at how stoned the boys were and started prodding them to make sure they were still alive. Hugo thought his time was up but managed to get back on his feet and roused his other three companions. The still laughing locals convinced them they didn't mean any harm. They just wanted to conclude the deal and send them on their way.

With their hard-won stash they bussed their way across to Kabul where they rented the top floor room of a hotel for two months. It was winter so they got a room that had an open fire. They had some great parties and always had the music blaring and friends visiting.

One night they had a big session and the smoke from continuous chillums filled the room, drifted into the corridors and billowed out into the street. The hotel manager came bashing on the door. He'd been tipped off the cops were on their way. The boys freaked out and started looking for places to hide their stash. One of them pulled the veranda pot plant out, put his stash below the soil and put the plant back on top. Hugo had his roughly sown into a green satin jacket that was hanging on the back of the door. One of the other guys hid his under the mattress while the last of them freaked out and threw his kilo on the fire where it smouldered and made the room a total stoner fog trap.

The cops turned up with rifles and somehow, in the haze, found the mattress stash and carted them off to the local jail where they were held for thirty days before facing the magistrate. The jail wasn't like anything in Australia. The cell doors weren't locked during the day but there was a really high fence around the compound, which was built around a giant tree with a chai shop underneath. Hugo had his money in his sock so he had cash to buy bedding, food and clean water. The shop sold everything you could need to pass the time including primo smoko and munchies. You could even buy a beer and a club sandwich from the local hotel if you had enough money.

There were about twenty foreigners sharing a big room and taking strength in their numbers against the other inmates. It was a free for all but there was one unwritten law and that was never

IN WALKED LUCK

go to the shower block alone as there were guys in that prison who'd been jailed for rape and murder.

During the day they would roll joints which they used as currency for their lockdown night-time card games. At the end of their thirty day spell the judge found them guilty and fined them whatever money they had left. He then released them back to their hotel which was exactly as they had left it. Hugo's kilo was hanging in his coat, and the "pot" plant bore fruit as well. They lit up a chillum to celebrate and promptly moved hotels to a quieter spot just outside of town.

While in Kabul, Hugo met Cookie for the first time, she was waiting for her boyfriend to get out of jail. Unfortunately, he was in for a long time as he was caught buying heroin. Hugo and Cookie then headed back to Paris resplendent in green satin, travelling off the hash and whatever money Cookie had left.

They travelled by bus through Iran and Turkey and planned to take a flight from Istanbul to Milano. There had been a plane bombing in Turkey so security was at an extreme level. After four body searches they sat in their plane seats only to have security arrive for one more search of the carry on luggage. After the police left and the seat belt signs lit up, Cookie turned to Hugo and said she was carrying some of the heroin that her boyfriend had slipped her. Hugo went white and was a nervous wreck for the rest of the flight and until Cookie offloaded it to a friend in Milano.

Back in Japan, Cookie and Hugo were off doing their thing, while Olga and I played at a resort on the west coast aboard a showboat that was moored near the town. We were kept aboard during this stint as there was nowhere else to go. The audiences were on some sort of tour. Probably a mix of golf and clubbing. It was a boring ten days but the money was really starting to pile up. Especially with the Saturday bonus. Sometimes when they had a really good night they would bring an envelope around and call it a "presento". More cash for the kitty, but nothing to spend it on - yet.

I was starting to feel like a crim carrying all that cash around. We would go to the bank whenever we could to swap some for larger denominations. In a few places we were able to buy one thousand U.S. dollars in travellers cheques. At other places we were able to transfer the yen to the equivalent of $US200 in cash.

Our next booking was in Fukuoka on the South Island. We were flown down there and met another couple who were new to the circuit. They were Americans just starting out so we helped them polish their act. The manager put us up in a love hotel. It was a crazy room with mirrors on the ceiling, a circular bed and a bar fridge to die for. The Americans, Annie and Phil, had a room as well. We had some good times away from the theatre, clubbing and sight seeing.

One night we were talking about how hard it was to get a smoko in Japan. Phil just so happened to have a small head he had carried in from Thailand. The only drama was there was no way of smoking it as we didn't have papers or a pipe. I thought about an Abdul but getting weed into an emptied cigarette is impossible as you can't get it fine or consistent enough. So I headed off down the street and found a tourist shop selling old tobacco pipes and bought one. It had a long stem and a tiny bowl. It looked stupid but we weren't going to let that stop us. The next hurdle was where to smoke it as the town folk were everywhere. In the end we found a small park and hid behind some bushes. It was a fun night laughing and recounting stories from previous adventures.

IN WALKED LUCK

On about day six the manager came in and told us to pack as he had been tipped off that they were about to be raided. We were as quick as lightning and had to duck-down in a cab heading for the airport.

Back in Tokyo we were put up in a small hotel for the remainder of that tour and left to our own devices. Finally we had a chance to explore some tourist sights and experience a traditional steam bath and scrub. We got to see the Royal Palace and the fish markets where we enjoyed a sashimi lunch in a restaurant with signs warning tourists that this wasn't going to be a cheap exercise. And it wasn't!

We picked up mail from the post office and there was a letter from Pedro. He was blown away that we were dancing and that I had taken his name. He said he had arrived back home looking like a bedraggled refugee from the hippie trail wearing wafer-thin cheese-cloth clothes, long hair and in need of a good meal. He was also "on the border line of mind". He was having trouble adjusting to the regimentation of the big city. He had to get a haircut, a shave and a job at the bar of the local golf club. It was a massive change of environment for Pedro and he was trying to fit in. He said grass was expensive, everyone smoked bongs, and they were listening to disco music. Apparently Abba were topping the music charts. He was horrified but was happy to hear the cicadas singing and to get to the beach whenever he could. He was saving for a motorbike!

When the next tour started we were ferried to another Tokyo venue. This time it was in the suburbs. There was nothing to do but hang out and read a lot. There was an American girl working on this roster that liked me. One day I was in the stage wings waiting to go on when she swayed up real close and started rubbing my crotch. Before I knew it she had me in her mouth. I only just managed to whip it out on my cue to go on stage. I think all were surprised, as I was glistening and ready for action from the outset. I spent the rest of the time at this venue trying to avoid my new friend.

At another venue we had to sleep in a large room with all the Japanese girls. Twice I woke to naked beauties snuggling in for some action. I didn't really want to go there but it was very difficult to resist when hands started wandering. I felt terrible as I loved Olga and didn't want to do anything to upset our relationship. I just wanted to move on to the next gig.

Larry then rang to say we were booked to go back to Sapporo. This time our French friends Cookie and Hugo would be there on their first double booking. We were looking forward as the theatre was the best we had experienced so far and it would be fun to have some familiar faces. When we finally got into Sapporo we only had a short time to catch up before we were on stage. Olga and I went first, and Hugo and Cookie followed. Hugo was scared shitless but with half a bottle of Suntory under his belt he rose to the occasion at all four sessions that day. To celebrate after the show we went to our hotel restaurant for dinner and a few drinks.

There was obvious tension between Cookie and Hugo. We figured it was the fact he ended up on stage, but as it came out there was a back story. Cookie had bought some heroin into Japan with her. She liked to smoke it, as did Hugo. Hugo was keeping it safe while Cookie was working. One day he left his wallet with the heroin in it on the counter of a department store. He didn't realise until he got back to the theatre. Given that his passport was also in the wallet he had to rush back to the shop to retrieve it. Not knowing how the situation would resolve itself, he enquired after the wallet and the shop manager took him into the back office and started asking him questions as to his identity. Hugo thought he was stalling and that the cops were coming, and he was envisaging all sorts of trouble, but the manager handed him the wallet with a smile and everything was intact. Amazingly the manager did not go any further than opening the passport. On his return Cookie let loose on Hugo and the bag went into the toilet.

Somehow twenty-one bottles of saki ended up on our table that night. Kanpai, kanpai, kanpai! We were shit faced and stumbled back to our rooms to lie down. I wasn't well and passed out. Sometime in the night I left the room to use the bathroom down the hallway. It looked like a typhoon had gone through the place. Someone had gone through a paper wall, the door to the bathroom was hanging off its hinges and there was spew everywhere. It wasn't me I was sure, but all I could do was crawl my way back to the room. We woke at about 11am with the worst of headaches, and ventured out to find tradesmen putting the final touches on the repairs to the hallway. In typical Japanese style the hotel never mentioned it and on our departure we handed over an envelope to show our gratitude.

It was a fun ten days with Cookie and Hugo. We became friends and at the end of it agreed that we would meet in Vientiane and take a villa there for a month so we could really relax in style.

Olga and I took on one more stint. It was in Tokyo. I think it was in the Roppongi district. It was very different from all the other gigs as there was a large American audience and they were really vocal. They gave me heaps of shit and were quite disrespectful to Olga. For some reason the daytime sessions were the worst but in the end I figured they were just jealous so we really hammed it up. We were careful not to leave the venue in case there were street encounters, but our visas needed renewal and with only days to spare we donned disguises and ventured to the embassy where we they stamped us good for another three months stay.

We couldn't believe we had been there for three months and on tour for ninety days straight. It was a pretty intense time living that lifestyle and we were getting pretty tired. We figured we'd done the act three hundred and seventy times and this last engagement hadn't been easy. So with a bag load of cash, almost forty grand, we decided to pull the plug before our luck ran out. The last thing we needed was to be deported and have our cash confiscated. We were also longing to hit the road and see where it took us.

We broke the news to Larry and at the end of that booking we met him and had a drink to celebrate. I think it was a record run for Larry so he couldn't really complain. He wished us luck and asked if we would keep an eye out for other willing couples. He promised to pay a commission if they came on board. And he let us keep the $US100 advance he had given us when we first arrived. He said it was a down payment.

We then headed to the tatami hotel where we had stayed on our first night in Japan. The hosts remembered who we were. It was probably Olga's hair. We booked a room for a week and they went into the back room to retrieve our backpacks. They were still there. Looking just as ratty but untouched. Everything was as we had left it. Imagine trying that anywhere else in the world.

That night we laid the money out on the floor before diving into it and doing the job in Japan one last time. We then split the money and stashed it so it was in smaller parcels. We put some in our gear, some on our body and the rest we put in our carry on luggage. It was only then that we realised exactly how much we had, and the possibilities that came with it.

The next morning we bought a ticket to Hong Kong and within days were on the road again. Bye bye Japan. What an adventure! At the airport I bought a watch to celebrate and traded some of our yen for Hong Kong and US dollars. We sweated when our cash went through the scanner but thankfully they didn't query it. On the plane we sat back in our seats with a giant sigh of relief. Did that really happen? I thanked the cards and held Olga's hand in a state of bliss and ordered two double gin and tonics.

CHAPTER SIX

Let The Good Times Roll

In Hong Kong we had some silk shirts made up and bought cheap tickets to Bangkok. We also changed cash, bought travellers cheques, and invested in money belts so we could keep it close to our bodies.

This time when we got to Bangkok we stayed in a much better tourist hotel. It was my twenty-first birthday and we were hanging out for a smoko. Olga went out to get something so we could celebrate. She came back with a big joint which she had bought from a random Thai guy just down the street. We went out into the hotel gardens and found a quiet spot to light up. My god, it was so strong that we could barely finish it…but we did. After sitting for a while and taking in the sunset and tropical plant-life we made our way back to our room and sat on the bed where, we watched the walls melt as we drifted off into a deep sleep. Happy birthday!

The next day we took an early morning train up to Udong Thani. We arrived about nightfall. We managed to get a small ferry boat across the river into Laos and then a taxi ride up to Vientiane and the Constellation Hotel.

When venturing out the next day we looked for the old cat, but he was nowhere to be seen. His shop was closed. We then looked around and found a villa that slept four and waited on Hugo and Cookie to arrive. They turned up about a week later and we spent the next month just relaxing.

The villa was about a kilometre outside of town in the jungle. It was a fortress – high fence, big gate, bars on the windows and doors. No electricity so it was candles at night. We were very out of it for the whole month thanks to some big opiated Buddha sticks from the growers market. The jungle noises at night were pretty wild or maybe it was our imagination. We slept with a kitchen knife close by and agreed to never answer the gate bell at night.

I was reading *The Politics of Heroin in South-East Asia*. It was written in the early seventies about the C.I.A. involvement in the Nugan Hand Bank and laundering money to buy heroin and ship it back to the States in U.S. Air Force planes from Vietnam. I couldn't believe the gall of the guys who put that scam together. It was big time.

It then came time to leave. Cookie and Hugo left the day before. They had to sort out visas in Bangkok. We were to meet them again in Kathmandu. Our river crossing into Thailand didn't quite go to plan as the Thai side of the border was closed. The ferryman decided we should try the next crossing which was about a kilometre up river. Thankfully it was open, so we disembarked. The Thai customs officials were immediately on our case, and despite the fact that the other crossing was closed, they were suspicious that we didn't use the main entry point. They didn't see a lot of westerners and wanted to check us out.

There were two guys and they ushered us into a small official building where they wanted to inspect our belongings. I had my backpack and a shoulder bag. Olga had a big cloth duffle bag. I also had a matchbox full of the leftover Buddha in my pocket. I just couldn't leave it behind. Olga knew what was coming and pointed to the river crossing outside. The two Thai guys and I looked out briefly as she quickly fished the matchbox out of my pocket and put it into hers. They turned back and started going through everything of mine including giving me a decent pat down. They even made me open my money belt. I got really nervous thinking they'd make a move to take it but they didn't.

They were harassing me over my camera and "that" book. They were insinuating I was C.I.A. and had been taking pictures. I could not have looked farther from the profile. At one point I thought I was going to have to give them the camera or at least the film to keep them happy. Then they left the room. Again, Olga knew what was going on and quickly put the matchbox back in my pocket, just before they came back with a woman who proceeded to give Olga a pat down and money belt check. Nothing to be found there. Thank God! After nearly two hours they let us go.

We walked like zombies into town and on to the bus station. We had narrowly escaped a very big drama. All for a matchbox of bloody grass. It definitely wasn't worth it. The bus ride was marked by a number of police stops and bus walk-throughs checking documents. After the second one I pulled the matchbox from my pocket and tipped the contents out the window as we were moving along. A sense of relief came across us and we held hands for the rest of the trip.

It was a long bus ride but, after passing a couple of thousand farms, we finally made it back to the crazy world that is Bangkok. We checked into the Grace Hotel and started organising the next leg. The plan was to get back to Kathmandu to catch up with Cookie and Hugo. We found a cheap flight on Thai Air and bought one-way tickets.

While waiting for our flight we met a number of travellers at the Grace and told a few of them about our escapades in Japan. One was a Hawaiian girl who was really interested, and the other an Australian couple that weren't so sure. The Aussies would have made a fortune. The guy looked like Conan the Barbarian and the girl like Zena the Warrior Princess. The guy was tanned, super muscular, had a barrel chest, long blonde hair, cropped beard and wore an open shirt to show his physique. He had a silver necklace with a pendant tight on his neck that could only be described as a hard penis with wings and two balls. It just bobbled and looked at you when he was talking. He had a great sense of humour. The girl was just as striking with muscles, long dark hair, big breasts and skimpy clothing. It was a fun few hours talking and looking at them. We handed out Larry's cards and wished them luck.

When we arrived back in Kathmandu it was a lot chillier than tropical Bangkok. Despite the cool it was a real treat to get back to the familiar sights and sounds of the small medieval town. We headed for the Post Office to see if there were any messages. There was an aerogram from Pedro and a message from Hugo saying they were staying at Swayambhu near the Monkey Temple.

We had tipped Pedro off when leaving Japan so he was across our plans to get back to Kathmandu. He was still working and was now living in a share house with friends. It sounded like they were drinking more than smoking. He had dusted off his surfboard and was getting to the beach as often as he could. At times he was hanging out with my cousin Johnny. He longed to get back out on the road and wished us luck.

Olga and I bought some woollen clothes and rented a room at the Oriental Lodge on Freak Street. The next morning we caught a bus out to see our friends. They were living in a house they had rented for a month. Cookie was entertaining dressmakers and Hugo was mulling up some fresh Nepalese hash. We had lunch with them, climbed the steps to the top of the Temple, and wrestled the monkey thieves. As we surveyed the view across the Himalayas we agreed we should do some trekking.

A week later we jumped on board the bus to Pokhara where we had ridden earlier on the pushbikes. We found a couple of nice rooms just outside the town. What a beautiful place. The rooms looked over the lake on one side and were surrounded by snow-capped mountains on the other. It was here Olga, Hugo, Cookie and I made ready for the trip ahead. We were going to take the

Annapurna track and go as far as we could. We knew very little. We had a hand-drawn map of the track with the villages marked along the way and hoped that we could last the ten days to Base Camp. We knew this would be our limit as we didn't have the kit to go any higher.

The thing about trekking in Nepal is there are lots of rivers in valleys and lots and lots of valleys. You have to cross them all as you make your way up into the ranges. The first days were spent working our way up the rugged river valleys. From six am through to about four pm we followed the riverbed. At some places we had to cross huge suspension bridges made of steel cable. As we got higher the bridges were made of rope and bamboo and they were wide and swayed … a frightening experience and really unnerving. On one crossing Hugo refused to go and only made it to the other side when an old village woman took him by the hand and guided him across. Then it started to get steeper. We spent hours walking up steps … thousands of them … and then hours walking down steps to get to the next valley. By steps I mean carved dirt and rocks through endless rice-paddy fields. All the time we were moving steadily upwards.

Come late afternoon we would enter a village to take chai and eat dahl and rice. We'd ask if they had a bed for the night and in most cases they did. We'd then sit around smoking chillums until it got dark and would be in bed by sunset.

On the second day the Canadian mountain boots that I had bought in the hiking store in Sapporo fell apart. The stitching that held the upper leather to the sole broke away making the boots impossible to wear. I ended up tying them together with rope so I could continue to wear them. I figured they must have been sitting around in that store for years and the stitching had become brittle. I didn't know what to do. It looked like my trip was over and I wasn't looking forward to going back all that way dragging the shredded boots. As we approached a village I showed my boots to some young boys. They pointed and one of them grabbed my arm so we followed. He led me to a cobbler who started stitching my boots with a giant needle and string. They were perfect after that.

For five days we headed up into the mountains. There was talk of bears and mountain cats but we didn't see any. The locals were very friendly and were keen to assist whenever we stopped to rest and repast. There were a few straight westerners walking the track. Apart from a happy hello we travelled without too much interaction. I don't think they would have liked our rest stops which were essentially finding a beautiful place to stoke up a chillum and take in the view. A few times we saw a group pass with older Europeans sitting in baskets on some Sherpa's back as they negotiated the never ending steps. How ridiculous and scandalous. It made us quite angry.

Our upward journey was now getting cooler and the track was starting to ice up. We got to Ghandruk village which was about thirty five kilometres out of Pokhara and about two thousand metres above sea level. The view of Annapurna and Machhapuchhare was unreal. They were right in front of us - sheer rock faces, snow, clouds and such amazing colours. We stayed in a small rest house which was about five kilometres away from the base camp … but it was another two thousand metre climb. Reluctantly we turned back. It wasn't easy as we were in heaven. It was so beautiful. The mountains rising in front of us and a view that went off into the never never behind us. The journey back took about four or five days. It felt a lot quicker as I think there is something about heading "home" rather than into the unknown.

After the trek it was pleasant to spend a few days in sunny Pokhara giving our feet and legs a rest. We spent our time reading, watching rural life around the lake, having cups of tea, talking to freaks, smoking joints and planning the next leg of our journey.

When we got back to Kathmandu we hit the post office and there was a letter from Annie and Phil, the couple we had met in Fukuoka. They were still doing "Hai Dozo" and had met up with the Hawaiian girl from Bangkok. She was having a ball and said she loved us. Olga and I had a good old laugh. We were happy we had kept Larry's hundred bucks.

Hugo and Cookie went back to their rented house and Olga and I got a nice room in town. We decorated the room with bits and pieces we had collected. We did lots of half-day walks into the countryside and got to know the backstreets of the town. We also hung out at our friend's house near the Monkey Temple where Cookie was always missing clothing and Hugo lost a few chillums. Damned monkeys! In the quiet times Olga focussed on her card readings and I explored the i-Ching.

After about a month we felt strong enough to go back down into India where the weather was getting cooler. We were keen to visit some ashrams that other travellers had told us about and Olga was keen to get down to Goa.

For the past year and a half we had been on the adventure of a lifetime, there was no plan, we just headed East until we couldn't go any further. We stumbled across money and we headed back to relive some of the adventures. I was starting to think about my family back home. My mum and dad, brothers and friends. I knew there was nothing happening at home as the correspondence was fairly regular but I wanted to see for myself. I had the money and wanted to connect with my family. I thought about it for a bit and talked to Olga. In the end it was agreed I would fly home for Christmas and join Olga, Cookie and Pedro in Southern India in a month's time.

To make sure I didn't get side-tracked I bought all the airline tickets. Kathmandu-Bangkok-Sydney-Kuala Lumpur-Madras. It was tough saying goodbye to Olga but she was very supportive and I knew Hugo would look after her. It was only for a month. I felt it wasn't such a big deal. I was just doing a side trip. Olga threw the tarot to read the story of our lives. Change was in the air but there was no big drama. I interpreted my I-Ching to say "bend with the breeze" and "treasure your home".

Olga and I had been through a lot as lovers and protectors. From that meeting aboard the ferry in Greece, through the madness of the hippie trail to India, the times in the Himalayas, crazy Thailand, dreamy Laos, Chinese Hong Kong, bizarre Japan, and our times with Cookie and Hugo. I felt like she was my soul mate and would be there for the long haul. I think she was a little disappointed that she wasn't coming on the Aussie leg but she didn't push it. There were lots of hugs and kisses at the airport and with mixed emotions I left her and passed through Immigration.

CHAPTER SEVEN

Welcome Home

It was two weeks before Christmas when I arrived in Sydney. I was travelling light and had nothing to declare so the process through customs went pretty quick. "Welcome home, just go through".

I was really glad to be back on Aussie soil. The feeling of stepping out into the huge blue Sydney sky was unique. I don't think I had seen a fully blue horizon sky since I had left. Everywhere I had been for the past year and a half the sky was grey from weather, seasons or pollution … or there were just glimpses of it from behind a mountain range or a city skyline. Australia is such a lucky country.

The flight came in at five thirty am so it must have been pretty early when I got out of the cab at my parent's house. I totally freaked them out. They were just getting up when I banged on the door. They couldn't believe it. No idea I was coming home, and very glad, until I told them I was just passing through.

BOM BOM

That afternoon I headed off to stay with my oldest brother who had just bought a grand, federation house that someone had turned into a grubby eight room dormitory. He was working long hours and had only had time to set up a few of the rooms. I got busy pulling the flats apart to get the house back to its original shell. It was pretty easy work as the walls were really flimsy, but there was a lot of rubbish so I called in a favour with our friend Mike who had a two door Kombi ute.

I remember briefing him on the front steps when a neighbour ran up asking if we owned a Volkswagen truck. Mike put his hand up and when he heard it had run off down the hill he immediately gave chase. Unbelievably it had got loose down a steep one way street, missed the parked cars on the left and buried itself between a telegraph pole and the fence. On the front seat was Mike's bag containing his home grown. It was such a lucky outcome as the alternatives could have been life changing. The cops turned up and Mike explained that there were schoolies in the street when he arrived and they might have set it free. He was positive he had put it in reverse and pulled the hand brake on. In the end the ute was drivable and there was no public damage so everyone counted their blessings. Mike sold the ute shortly after but from then out he always took an extras thirty seconds to make sure his cars were safe and secure.

Once the rooms were liberated my brother's girlfriend and our cousin Johnny moved in, and we had lots of fun and some great house-warming parties.

On my second day back I caught up with Pedro. For old times sake he arrived wearing his Afghan gear. He laughed loudly and we had a great time reliving some of our crazy experiences. He was in a good place which was great to see. No bike yet, but it was coming.

WELCOME HOME

I caught up with lots of other friends on this layover. I rode motorbikes, smoked Aussie bush grass, went to the beach a lot, and used the stay as an opportunity to get a simple kit together for the next leg of the trip. I also saw some great music.

The best was *AC/DC* at the Hordern Pavilion. Naturally we were ripped when we went in and we were literally blown away. It's such an intimate venue and the audience were a part of the whole experience as Bon Scott was screaming, Angus and

Malcolm Young thrashed their guitars, Mark Evans drove the bass, and Phil Rudd belted out on drums. It was so loud. I came away feeling like my whole body had been assaulted. Every cell was ringing. An awesome set of favourites. They were the number one hard rock band in the world ... even if they hadn't yet been crowned.

Life was good back in Australia. The Labour government had been spending money flat out and people were positive. Sadly, but expectedly, the money had just run out and the government got caught trying to do a dodgy loan deal, so the Governor General of the day had them sacked and put his Liberal party in power. There was talk that the Queen had told him to do it. Needless to say the Republican movement demanded we dump the Commonwealth ... and Mr Murdoch's press was having a field day. A lot of interesting machinations emerged to change politics forever. Optimistically, it spawned the Australian Marijuana Party whose mission was to legalise marijuana. Writer JJ McRoach was the lead candidate for the Senate and amazingly he was just a few votes short of being elected. Their campaign line resonated – "Plant a Dope in Canberra".

Before I knew it, it was time to leave. It felt like it had been a really short stay but on reflection I had done a lot. I still had a fair bit of money - more than I would need for this trip - so I figured I'd leave some behind for when I returned. I found a great hiding place at my brother's house and figured I could always call him if I needed it to be sent.

Some of my family and friends came to the airport to say goodbye. It was the thing friends did back in those days. When the call came for my Malaysian Airlines flight I managed to hug everyone, waved, and disappeared into the airline gate ... and the unknown. I was ready for India. I had a small shoulder bag containing a sarong, a pair of swimmers, a change of undies, a second shirt, a pair of shorts and my toiletries including Aspirin, Dettol, paw paw cream, gauze, tape and Lomotil. I didn't have a lot else as I knew that when my things got dirty I could wash them and they'd be dry within the hour. I was really, really looking forward to seeing Olga.

CHAPTER EIGHT

Blowing In The Wind

Kuala Lumpur was my stopover. It was just for one night and then I would take a plane on to Madras (now Chennai). Malaysia was a heavy place. There were signs everywhere about the death penalty for drugs. They had a big heroin problem as it was a distribution point for shipments coming out of the Golden Triangle (the border area of Laos/Burma/Thailand). After cleaning up the big time traffickers at the ports, the authorities were working on the dealers on the streets. I was determined to stay straight … that was until I walked out of my hotel and the first guy I met offered me weed. What could I say? It was just a joint. So I asked him for a light and smoked it immediately. No evidence. Stoned, I turned around and went back to my hotel room and fell into a deep sleep. It was the best sleep I'd had in ages. The room was dark, quiet and I was tired after my flight.

I woke up late and had to rush to get back to the airport to catch my plane. I was really starting to get excited. Madras and

Olga were just hours away. I was hanging out to see her and tell her of my Aussie adventures. I'd always felt a little embarrassed about the scene in Sydney being too colloquial but after this trip I really appreciated it for what it was. I vowed to take Olga back with me next time.

The plane landed and taxied to a stop on the runway. I sat trying to see out the window and was struck by the fear of no one being there to meet me. I knew I was in the hands of the Gods. I was hoping it was Ganesh, the good luck elephant boy.

The airport was a free for all. I walked down the flight stairs into a crowd that were meant to be behind the rope barricade. I couldn't see Olga anywhere. It was just a sea of Indian faces. Then I saw something familiar. It was Hugo yelling and waving his arms like the Frenchies do. He was a sight - dressed in an open silk Hawaiian shirt, a sarong, Japanese split-toed work boots and his long flowing hair. It was a great re-union. Lots of kissing and hugging. In the huddle I was trying to look around to see who else was there when Hugo said that Olga wasn't coming.

"She's gone baba, she met a German guy in Kathmandu and has gone off travelling."

What was it about German guys? I was shattered. After everything we had been through. I couldn't believe it. It was only a month. There was a big chunk of my heart missing and I felt like I was in a daze until Hugo slapped me and said: "Fuck the chicks. Let's go."

Apparently Cookie had bailed on him as well and was heading back to Japan. They were still friends but she had to go. There was a scam waiting. I was pretty freaked knowing Olga was with someone else and was trying to work out if I hadn't made it clear I was coming back. Did she meet that German guy from Hong

BLOWING IN THE WIND

Kong again? My mind was racing. She didn't even write me a letter. I hoped she was OK.

Hugo couldn't believe how light I was travelling. Getting through customs was quick. We went to the airport train station, bought a ticket and jumped onto the next train to the main city station. We were having a great time until the conductor came around to check tickets. He was carrying on about something and we weren't listening. It finally became apparent that we were in the first class carriage and we had second class tickets. The bloody conductor wasn't going to let it go and when we got to our destination he escorted us to the stationmaster's office. It was a long room with a "very important" man sitting at the end of a long desk. It was like being in court. We didn't want to exacerbate the situation, so we were very respectful, apologetic and sought forgiveness. The stationmaster bought our story of it being an exuberant re-union, asked us to pay the difference in fares, and waved us off.

Hugo had a room at the Dasaprakash Hotel in town. I took a room there as well. It was low key, clean and private. We were having a Duty Free scotch and some great Afghani hash in his room when an American girl Hugo had met earlier that day dropped around. She was a small brunette called Belle and she had a tall blonde friend called Liz with her. It wasn't long before the Johnny Walker Black and half a dozen joints were consumed and we were heading off to bed. Liz and I went back to my room and Belle stayed on with Hugo. What an awesome way to forget my earlier woes. Liz was hot. A beautiful calm person with the best body. It was a great night as we chatted between cuddles and joints.

Liz was the best thing that could have happened to me at that time. She was an Aries and relaxed about everything. She was really sexy. Tanned and athletic from playing tennis, she wore skimpy lacy knickers and her body hair was very short. Like most girls at the time she didn't wear a bra and loved flowing dresses where she could let it all be loose underneath. She was studying law back home in the States so she was pretty smart. She thought she'd ultimately drop out as it was too stressful. She really liked me. I felt six feet tall.

The week we were in Madras was a lot of fun. We explored the city and went to the Sri Aurobindo Ashram in Pondicherry. Sri Aurobindo was an early supporter of an independent India and had begun the practice of Yoga. Following a spiritual realisation he withdrew from politics and went to Pondicherry where, with the help of his spiritual collaborator, the Mother, founded the Ashram. Its aim was to liberate one's consciousness. After about forty years of spiritual practice he left his body and also left a legacy for all.

After hanging around the Ashram for a while, and learning some basic yoga and meditation techniques, we headed to the beach to watch the entire village net-fish together. It was incredible to see everybody doing their small part in what was a highly evolved activity. After the nets were dragged in and the fish had been divided, we were invited by a fisherman to share his catch.

His hut was in the sand hills. It was one room, made of mud, and we squatted around the fireplace while his wife and daughter prepared and cooked the tiny fish in a coconut curry. It was delicious. These were poor people but they had huge hearts and were happy with their lives. They were dark skinned, almost black, probably part-heredity and part-living on the beach in a sarong all their lives. We communicated in the most basic way but the conversation was meaningful. We left a little cash present and parted ways.

The next morning one of the girls found some acid she'd brought in from the States. She thought she'd lost it. We took it and started wandering around the streets. The trip took forever to come on and we were getting hungry, so we decided to have some lunch. We spied an Italian restaurant. So, keen to try something that wasn't curry and rice, we ordered spaghetti which turned out to be noodles and tomato ketchup. Really revolting! As we were sitting there the acid came on and before long the single cockroach that was walking up the wall became a moving wallpaper of the vile insects. It was time to leave.

As we stumbled out of the restaurant we saw a carnival down the street. I could hear motorbikes roaring. We went to check it out. There was a giant timber structure consisting of long planks of wood standing on their ends, tied together with rope into a large cylinder. The sign read: 'Wall of Death'. The engine noises were coming from inside. It was too much. We had to check it out. "Four tickets please!" We followed the queue and were soon climbing timber steps strapped to the outside of the cylinder. They ended in a plank that hung to the outer rim on the top of the ten metre high barrel. There was a rope in front of us to hold on to. We peered in. There he was! A middle-aged Indian rocker with an open-chested red satin shirt, black jeans and boots sitting on a really clapped out BSA 250.

All seemed OK at first. We were tripping but were under control. Just lots of giggling and excitement. Then the rider put his bike into gear, revved it up and dropped the clutch. The noise reverberated up through the structure and our bodies. He was soon riding around the dirt mound and then the base of the timber ring. Then all of a sudden the entire structure started swaying as he began climbing up around the wall. We held on to the rope as tight as we could. We dreaded each time he passed as it flung our section of the wall out. We were only hanging on by the rope and our feet that gripped the plank. The faster the rider went the greater the movement. Soon he was riding the rim with no hands, his feet on the handlebars, and his red shirt blowing in the wind. He was just centimetres from the lip. The crowd ducked every time he passed. People were screaming. We were off our brains. The whole thing was tied together with rope! It was ridiculous. We couldn't get off it and we couldn't wait until it was over. The timbers stretched the ropes on each pass. The G-Forces were incredible and it was one of the most frightening things I had ever experienced. Maybe the whole thing was heightened by the acid but when it was over we were lolly-legged, jibbering messes and had to sit on the ground outside the sideshow for thirty minutes while we recovered … with a very strong cup of chai.

As we walked back to the hotel the traffic and the crowd became more dense and someone bumped into me quite hard. I didn't really take much notice at the time but when I got back to my hotel I noticed the side of my shoulder bag had been slashed with a razor blade. I had my valuables in the bag and would normally have pushed the bag around in front of my chest when in a crowded situation. Thankfully it was double-lined and nothing fell out. I had the bag repaired with a tough canvas patch and kept it under my shirt from then on out. I considered myself very lucky as the street kids normally got what they wanted.

Belle was keen to go on to Kathmandu and Hugo was keen to be her tour guide. I didn't want to go as it would have bought back too many memories, and I really did want to check out southern India. Thankfully Liz wanted to stay with me. The next day we parted ways. Hugo and Belle flew to Nepal. Liz and I took a bus to Trivundrum. Southern India is Hindu and the temples got crazier with cartoon-like, brightly coloured statues of the gods, carved on top of each other in an array of tantric positions. The food also got hotter, and the people more friendly.

Liz and I were having a great time. I found that she was separated from her husband and things hadn't been good for quite a while. She enjoyed making up for the sex she had missed out on, and I was well-seasoned from Japan to go six times a day if required. We tried to re-enact all the Hindu Temple love-making carvings and explored lots of deeply physical and meditative tantric positions. It was amazing that we managed anything but the inside of our hotel rooms.

As we went further south it got very rural and we saw very few travellers. I think this finally got to Liz as it had become a hard slog and was no longer a sight seeing trip. She was longing to get back home and soon said goodbye. It was a sad day when I put her on the train that would take her across the entire sub-continent to Bombay (now Mumbai) where she could catch a flight back to the States. I was worried as she had to travel thousands of miles on crowded trains alone and endure the crazy heat of the Indian summer, but I couldn't change her mind.

After she left I felt quite empty. I didn't know what to do next. I was going to miss her vibrancy and friendship. But I was close to the bottom of India and that was where I was heading. It is really something to be traveling alone in off-the-track areas. I didn't see another traveller for about two weeks and didn't have a real conversation with anyone for the same time. I practiced meditation every chance I got. Sometimes sitting for hours trying to clear my mind only to find it got more cluttered. Eventually I surrendered to the fact that I couldn't clear my head and it was then I had my most lucid thoughts. I reflected on my original journey from home, my adventures, going home again and now being in no man's land. There was no Olga so why was I there. I felt I needed to play out this hand of cards, as I may not ever get another opportunity to test my own resolve. If there was ever a time to roll the i-Ching coins this would have been it, but they were back in Australia.

As planned I arrived at Cape Comorin, an old English port and the southern-most point on the sub-continent, on the full moon. There was a temple on the beach. It was the Bagavarthi Temple dedicated to Shiva. There were all sorts of pilgrims and sadhus from all over India and it was a very spiritual experience. I made a nice strong chillum and ceremonially puffed away as the moon was coming up over the water of the Arabian Sea, the Indian Ocean and the Bay of Bengal.

The temperature and the food in southern India are both very hot! I think the food was designed to be hot so you sweat and whatever breeze there is has a cooling effect. In Tamil Nadu state meals are typically a range of small tasting dishes served on banana leaves. Most of the meals are Hindu vegetarian. Rice and dahl (dried mung beans) are the staples to which they add side plates of eggplants, gourds, curries and lentils. Green chilies, cloves, cardamom, coconut, onion and garlic are used to spice things up. Marsala Dosai, or thin pancakes fried in ghee and wrapped around a filling of spicy potato and vegetable, were my favourite. Followed by a cold yoghurt lassi drink, and a hot chai which was spiced with everything and poured with spectacular flourish. Every chai baba had a technique to pour the tea. Some from intricate old tea pots to glass cups which were held some two metres away. They were real showmen.

BLOWING IN THE WIND

The southern most tip of India was a meeting point and playground for Hindu Sadhus. There were babas expressing their devotion in a bewildering variety of ways. There were long-haired chillum babas who smoked ganga to Shiva; naked babas who owned nothing but their cooking pots; babas that tied weights to their penis and had to roll it up so they could move around; babas who lived in caves and didn't speak; and even a baba I heard about who rolled instead of walking. His name was *Lotan Baba*. He had a very worn leather cape to protect his skin. He had rolled sideways (from where I was standing that night at the most southern tip of India) all the way up to Kashmir some three thousand kilometres away. All in the name of peace. He could even smoke a cigarette as he rolled. He gave a whole new meaning to "smoking a rollie". Apparently when he was in his early teens he stood in one place for seven years and only ate grass. Mad! It's amazing what the human body can endure.

Bus travel was pretty much the only way you could move around but, on a few occasions, I hitched a ride in a truck. It was a real trip being up in the cabin with two or three drivers. They all helped. One steered, one operated the clutch and one changed gears. Their conversations were loud over the deafening engine noise. The interior decorations needed to be seen to be believed. Every square centimetre of the cabin was painted or brass-plated and there were dangling objects in every space. All celebrating the Gods, who they hoped were watching over them.

The buses were decorated with similar enthusiasm and were reliable, cheap, but slow. Most came out of the Tata factory, India's answer to the Ford Motor Company. On a typical journey you pottered along a bumpy road at about ten kilometres an hour. Typically the doors, windows and sometimes the roof were open. You felt like you were passing through the landscape on an Adventureland ride.

My next journey was up to Thiruvananthapuram* in Kerala state on the west coast. And then, I thought perhaps I would make my way up to the ultimate hippie hang out at Goa. Thiru* was a seaside town jam-packed with coconut palms much like the rest of the state. It had lots of lagoons and waterways and was a coastal trading hub. I took a small room close to the beach and went for a swim. While sitting on the beach I was propositioned to buy ganga. I was almost out of Hugo's hash and needed to replenish. The young boy who was selling said it would cost me the equivalent of two dollars, so I said yes. I had some idea what that might buy and it would probably get me by for a few days. He came back about ten minutes later with a shoe box under his arm and opened it to reveal it was full of great big heads. It was enough for a month or two! I didn't like travelling with anything that I couldn't put in my pocket – not that it would have been a problem in the depths of Kerala, but when on a bus the last thing I needed was a shoe box full of heads. The stink would have sent the mothers and babies crazy and been a magnet for the cops.

The kid fired up a chillum to demonstrate its quality. As we smoked I realised this was super strong weed. I was off my tree and started to get paranoid so I grabbed a handful of the stuff and told the kid to keep the rest. He thought I was crazy, but eventually he walked off to sell it to the next silly long hair.

I stayed in town for a few more days, checking out the local sights and trying to work out where I would go next. It was an interesting place with lots of Portuguese and Dutch trading history evident in the architecture and the food. The ganga really helped me appreciate the surroundings and helped me make up my mind, I was going to avoid Goa and head to the Maldives instead.

...I arrived at Cape Cormorin where I packed a nice strong chillum and ceremonially puffed away as the moon came up over the water of the Arabian Sea...

Goa was too much of a scene, a lot of hippies and international Gucci travellers getting their bohemian fix. There were also lots of desperate people, crime, and the drugs were hardcore. I thought it was likely that Olga was there but I didn't want to be the guy that was always looking, and what if I found her? At the end of the day she had gone off with someone else. I was happy that she was happy and thankful for the awesome experience we shared. Mind you, replacing her beauty and open spirit wasn't easy.

The Maldives were pretty unknown at the time. I couldn't find a travel agent that knew anything about getting there and what was there once you arrived. And Thiru was probably the closest Indian port. I think the locals were a bit indifferent because it was a Muslim country. The stars weren't aligning. I had grown fond of the Hindu way of thinking. They just took every day for what it was and threw their hands up about the future. They had a good time God for everything and most were happy with their lot in life.

The word I was getting was that Sri Lanka (Ceylon) was a great place to hang out. It was a combo of Hindu, Buddhist and Christian and a lot more chilled than the Maldives. It also had surf. So I was in.

It was good to be getting out of India as there is only so much you can handle at a time. There are so many people and it is so hot. I managed to get a good deal on a flight. I hadn't heard of the airline before but thankfully the trip was uneventful. Coming into Colombo we circled a few times and got a low-flying bird's eye view of the place before landing. The British influence was there in a unique, architectural way. Churches, government buildings, fortresses and some classy looking colonial residences.

I decided not to stay in Columbo but to head straight to the beach. I made my way on foot from the airport to the colonial-style railway station. It felt a little like being in a ghost town after India. There were a lot less people trying to get a piece of you. They just got on with their own business.

It was a short wait for the slow train south to the beachside town of Hikkaduwa. It was slow because periodically it would stop in a slip rail for 30-45 minutes to allow another train to complete its journey on the same single track. The train was crowded and it was really hot. I had to breathe slow and deep to keep calm. This situation wasn't helped by the fact that I was standing, and a coconut water seller, using a machete, was hacking at coconuts which he held high above people's heads. Any swipe could have opened the wrong coconut.

BLOWING IN THE WIND

Finally, I arrived at Hikkaduwa, a small fishing village on the west coast, where the breeze was cool and salty. Such a refreshing feeling. I walked south from the train station along the beach road until I saw a room rental sign. It was a quiet walk with no touts pushing to buy, sell, rent, give or fuck. I liked it.

The room was located in a single level house and it had its own entry. There were three other rental rooms. All were sparsely furnished, clean and cool. The house was on a large block which had coconut trees, and bananas and paw paws in abundance. The grounds were covered in a lush grass that various domesticated animals nibbled and poo'd on. The owners (grandmother, husband, wife and two kids) lived in the kitchen area at the back of the house. They were a beautiful Buddhist family and very respectful of one's personal space.

On the property behind a clump of palms was an open-air well for bathing. You just threw the bucket down about twenty feet into a clean, icy cold well. After long days on the beach it was the most welcome of rituals – invigorating the whole body. The toilet was also outside. It was a long drop and very clean.

The beach was twenty-five metres away on the other side of the road. Under the strip of coconut palms leading to the sand was a small one room bamboo and palm-covered shack where a couple of Aussie surfer guys were living the dream - waves and bongs. It was the only shack on the beach and had a concrete floor with two bunks. Not very secure but, as I discovered, there was no local crime. Most things could be left out in the open and they would be there when you got back.

About twenty metres away and under the palms was a canary yellow 1960s Morris van that had been an ambulance in another life. It was now a motor home. Inside lived a pommie couple in their late thirties who has driven from the UK. They had enjoyed a long period of touring the world as cooks for an international rock band and its entourage. John and Michelle were old hippie stoners who had loaded up a couple of kilos of the best gold-stamped black Afghani hash on their way through and now had it stashed in a special compartment behind the fridge. They were cool people with lots of rock'n'roll stories. We became good friends.

The Aussie surfers also became good mates. When they weren't wearing board shorts they were in sarongs. Long, long blonde hair, beards and their bodies ripped from a life of surf. They were hard-core, cone-pulling heads who had crafted a big bamboo bong that must have been two-foot-high. It held a ceremonial place on the only shelf in their hut. They mostly smoked grass and would easily smash twenty or so cones each ... every day. They were funny guys, infectious with their enthusiasm for the water and the waves it dished up. They were from the Shire - the beachside suburbs of southern Sydney. And if ever there were a couple of guys who would fit right into a *Captain Goodvibes* comic it was them. *Snort, snort!*

In the front room of the house was an American girl from the mid-west who was enjoying some quiet time. She read a lot and enjoyed playing her country-rock music up loud. She was just an acquaintance until one day she asked me to come inside for tea. She then started playing the track '*Love The One You're With*' and things progressed from there. She was a bit too cosmic for me so I didn't go back. Funnily one day the Aussie boys were talking about how they too had been seduced and how she had played the same track. I laughed thinking about how many times I had heard Stephen Stills belt out that song when I was in my room.

BLOWING IN THE WIND

Hikkaduwa turned out to be great town. Not too many travellers. The locals were good and the surf was great. I spent a lot of time in the water, catching waves and skin diving over the coral reefs. When I wasn't in the water I was hanging out at a tea shack behind the coconut trees. They had a great way of doing their fried eggs and would drop them in some sort of syrup whip that formed a crispy shell that you broke back into the egg. The tea was also great - fresh tips from the nearby mountains with condensed milk. They also did awesome jaffles, had local cakes and it was all very cheap. If you wanted fruit there was an abundance of coconuts, paw paws and bananas. Most of the time you just picked them and ate. The locals were a bit funny about the coconuts as I think their land tax was based on the number of trees on their property and the earnings potential.

I saw all sorts of beachfront action. Lots of naked Germans, Italians and Frenchies and the occasional conservative Japanese couple; lots of chillum smoking; and lots of locals ogling the scene. A mini-Goa! On more than one occasion I had to save someone from the surf or pull out my trusty bottle of Dettol to flush coral cuts. I had lots of "owe-you-my-life" friends and was invited to parties and smokos.

After a month of this I was keen to see more of Sri Lanka so I hired a motor bike and set out to ride around the island. It was a twin cylinder Honda which was a special bike. The locals had mostly old British singles so I got a lot of envious looks. They also noticed me because I rode with my headlight on to make sure they could see me coming. They saw me and couldn't understand why anyone would have their lights during the day. Most of the locals didn't even turn their lights on at night.

Kandy was going to be my first destination. It was up in the hills. The road up was windy and there were lots of trucks and a blancmange of cars, bikes and bicycles. It was a challenge. I hadn't ridden a bike in the craziness of the subcontinent before. I was amazed I survived. As I climbed it got colder. By the time I got to the top I was frozen and could hardly keep my fingers working the levers. I ended up with a head cold so I holed up in a small hotel and sipped hot teas for a couple of days. This was the tea capital of the world and I enjoyed tasting lots of different types.

Kandy is a beautiful town set around a lake. Gems and semi-precious stones seemed to be the town's main commercial activity. I learnt a lot about stones after I showed some interest in a shop window. Within seconds I was whisked inside to be shown their merchandise along with a long explanation of each between a couple of rounds of tea and sweets. I didn't have any money (for stones) and I think they eventually accepted that, but they weren't going to miss the opportunity to show off their most precious pieces which they fetched from their deepest safes. Some of these stones were the size of pigeon eggs and hallucinatingly beautiful.

Next stop was Arugam Bay, a surfing tourist resort on the east coast. It was a good day's ride and an unforgettable arrival as I rode around the foreshore of the palm-lined bay at sunset. There I found a nice looking hotel on the beachfront with a jungle backdrop.

After getting my room sorted, I enjoyed tea in the lounge area while waiting for the restaurant to open. It turned out that there were no other guests and there was no electricity. As night settled in they lit a few lamps around me but they didn't waste fuel on the other areas. I could only see the one room I was in.

The silence of the night crickets was broken with shouting from the kitchen. The cook and the manager were having a barney. The chef then appeared in the doorway with a giant meat cleaver and raced towards me shouting. I shit myself and retreated a couple of feet. I made sure there were a few tables between us. He was raving mad, and I feared for my life as he was swinging the bloody cleaver around like a maniac. Eventually I realised from his gesturing that he was telling me his side of the argument and didn't mean me any harm. Even so I didn't hang around for dinner and went straight (feeling my way) to my room and, after lighting a candle, I bolted the door and leaned bits of furniture against it. I didn't sleep that night and was glad to leave early the next morning after unloading on the manager.

On my next leg I ended up in a wildlife park where I parked my bike at the Information Hut and boarded the tour bus. The group saw all sorts of animals including wild elephants up close. On dusk we arrived back at the hut where the other passengers were shuttled back to their hotels in cars. Once everyone had left, I stoked up a joint and took in the atmosphere and the noises.

Almost without warning it started to rain so I got back on my bike and headed down the dirt track towards the main road entrance. The rain was coming down quite hard and there were a million bugs flying around and hitting me in the face. I half shut my eyes to help see the track ahead. Within minutes I was face-to-face with a herd of wild buffalo. They were heading towards me and there was high grass on either side of the track. I had to keep going straight into the herd. There was about twenty of them. I don't know how I did it, but I managed to manoeuvre the bike around their legs and horns. They let me pass without getting spooked and I was out the back and had a clean path to the road. Maybe my headlight hypnotised them? Wow that was close!

I stopped at a colonial rest house for the night and got some weird looks from the guests and staff. When I got to my room and looked in the mirror I could see why. My face was covered in rain splattered dust and bugs and my glasses had left two clean saucer eyes. A hot bath, dinner and a welcome night's sleep followed as I tried to forget the buffalos and the cook and cleaver episode.

Over the next few days I continued up the north east coast through Kulmunai and Batticaloa to Trincomalee and, finally, Jaffna. Trincomalee and Jaffna were highly militarised. I could feel a strange undercurrent in the hotels as there were a lot of suss-looking international businessmen sitting around in the foyer. A few years later a full-scale war broke out as Tamil Indians (The Tamil Tigers) who were settled in the area fought for an independent state. The war lasted nearly fifty years, as they used a combination of guerrilla warfare and suicide bombers to take out Sri Lanka's strategic infrastructure and Buddhist temples.

Thankfully the Singhalese government won and these days the area is a vibrant fishing and tourist district.

It had taken me about ten days to circle the island and I was back in Colombo where I was approached by lots of men asking whether I had anything to sell. They wanted clothes, appliances, watches, in fact anything western. I struck up a conversation with one guy and he offered to take me to a private club in a large colonial hotel. What a scene that was! It was a throwback in time. There were starched uniforms offering me drinks and towels. "Sorry I can't remember my room number." I ended up having a refreshing swim and an interesting conversation with a Swiss couple who were there consulting on hotel business.

...at Anuradhapura I visited the descendant of Buddha's Fig Tree,.. of which, it is said He sat under and gained Enlightenment...

Colombo was the last stop before heading back down to sleepy Hikkaduwa. I felt a huge sense of achievement handing back the bike un-scratched and knowing I had ridden on those crazy roads without falling off once. I was keen to tell my tale to John and Michelle, so with celebratory joints I told them of my adventures and how, perhaps one day, I would return with a truck load of western goods to sell to the locals.

I thought a bit more about selling western goods to the locals and figured it was just a quick trip to Singapore where I could load a couple of suitcases. I hadn't been to Singapore before and the flights were cheap. After doing some numbers, I worked out that there was a really good chance I could double or triple my money. No-one wanted to come with me, so I bought the tickets and started making a list of potential purchases.

The flight was leaving from Colombo. John volunteered to drive me up. We arrived in the city on the evening before my flight. John was keen to check out an opium den, so he asked some guys who led us down some seedy backstreets. It definitely did not feel like a good idea. They came through though. Next thing we knew was we were smoking a few pipes and it was getting close to dawn. I don't know how it happened but, somehow, John drove me to the airport and I caught my flight for Singapore.

I slept through the flight and woke just as we landed. With just hand luggage I was standing in the queue ready to go through immigration when I put my hand on my pocket and felt the tola of hash that John had given me the day before. I'd forgotten all about it. It was supposed to be for my smoking pleasure but I went white thinking about the death penalty signs that were posted above my head.

It was my turn with the immigration guy. Thankfully he wasn't interested in anything other than my hair. It was too long for Singapore. He pointed to a poster that showed men's hair needed to be above the collar. He then gave me a pair of scissors and pointed to the bathrooms. I went in and lined up in front of the mirror with half a dozen other guys all doing a bad job of hacking their hair. It was a funny sight.

I was paranoid about what was in my pocket but I didn't dare chuck it out in case it was discovered. I returned to Immigration, he looked at my hair, stamped my passport, and told me to get a proper haircut in town. He gave me a document that had to be signed by the barber and handed in at a police station within two days. The police had to counter stamp my passport.

With just a wave through I cleared Customs, caught a tourist bus into town, sought out some cheap accommodation, and that night visited Boogie Street. It's gone now, but what a crazy place it was back then. Open air restaurants where all the patrons sat on the street watching the passing parade of locals, all dressed up to satisfy someone's sexual preference. Lots of ladyboys and everything in between. A real eye opener and a big laugh.

Next day I went to a barber shop and got them to shorten my hair at the back. There was still plenty on top which I could slick down. I then visited the cop shop and got them to endorse my passport. I was right to leave the island without a fine or jail time.

The tola was burning a hole in my pocket. I had to smoke it but you just couldn't smoke anything. There were people everywhere. In the end I crumbled it onto peanut butter sandwiches and got twice as shit-faced. I was out of it for a week while I shopped. Bargaining while you are stoned can be fun. No inhibitions and no time restraints. I was in for a chat, and happy for some civilised tea ceremonies and plenty of long haul negotiations. If I was going to sell stuff back in Sri Lanka, I knew I had to get it at a good price.

Buying multiple goods from the one retailer is the best way to negotiate. I started out asking about a particular shirt and then I would add a range of colours. Then I'd ask for some ties to match and, maybe, some cufflinks, some pants, a belt or two or three, matching jackets, sunglasses to suit a number of looks, watches and more. The shop keepers couldn't believe it as I kept adding to the pile. I was smart enough to stop every now and then and ask for a discount on the volume. And then later get a discount on that discount.

One evening I fell asleep after a peanut butter dessert and woke to see a big rat on the sideboard next to my bed. I startled it, and it leapt across my face, scratching my cheek with its claws. It landed on the window sill and disappeared between the bars outside. I let out a scream and ran for the trusty bottle of Dettol. I scrubbed my face, closed the window, and tried to sleep. No one came to see what the screaming was about and it wasn't mentioned the next day. The scratches were there so I knew I hadn't been dreaming.

Thinking about waking to danger, I remember a story a mate told me of his business trip to Hong Kong where he stayed in a top notch hotel. He was a cigarette smoker and a drinker. One night he woke to a room full of smoke and the fire brigade breaking down his door. His mattress was smouldering and as he leapt off the bed, he left behind a white silhouette on blackened bedsheets. A few minutes longer and he would have ignited. He was thrown out into the street with his luggage and a badly burnt credit card.

I eventually arrived back in Colombo with a suitcase full of clothing, perfume, sunglasses, watches, cameras and a stereo in a briefcase. You just flipped the briefcase open to reveal a turntable, cassette deck, amp and speakers. All good things that I knew I could sell for a profit. No dramas through customs as I dressed in some of the gear and looked like the business.

BLOWING IN THE WIND

When I arrived back in Hikkaduwa they were shell-shocked after a big bust. John told me how twelve cops turned up and started hassling all the travellers. They were looking for a John and some other guy called Steven. Somehow, he was on their list and they wanted to check him out. John took the British stance and tried to intimidate them, which worked to some extent, but didn't win him any friends.

They wanted to see his passport so he went into his van and just locked the door behind him. He quickly hid his stash in the "special" compartment. By this time the cops were banging on the door and when he let them back in, he said the lock had jammed. They were angry but didn't find anything. How lucky for him and for me not being there. I just had some smoko but didn't need the drama of them intimidating my Buddhist landlords while they tipped the place upside down. The bummer was the cops were onto our little paradise. So it was time to go.

I thought I would try to catch up with my mate Hugo in Kathmandu and then head home after that. John and Michelle were also on the move. They were going to start the return drive to the UK via Kathmandu and invited me along as a way of defraying the fuel costs. I figured it would be a different way of seeing the east coast of India so I went along for the ride, even though my share of the fuel would probably cost me more than a flight.

I had some success offloading my bits and pieces from Singapore. The rest I knew I could sell in India. We told a few of the locals that we were moving on and they said there was money to be made with the clove spice. Funny the East India Company was set up in the year 1600 to trade in Spice and here it was four hundred years later and it was still a thing. Those smelly little buds were worth a lot in India but to buy them at the right price meant going up to Kandy. So, John and I caught the bus to Kandy and bought five kilos each. They were big bags and they definitely smelt of Cloves. What a stink! John put his in a cupboard in the van. I wrapped mine in plastic and made it look like a backpack.

The day came to leave. It was sad. What a beautiful beach holiday. We drove slowly up to Mannar, an old Portuguese port north of Colombo, where John put the van on an open, wooden ferry that took about ten cars. The customs out of Sri Lanka was almost non-existent which was good. As we got closer to Rameshwarum in India we weren't sure what to expect. The only thing we knew was that the cloves had a very strong smell. Not something you could disguise. It started to feel like it was not a smart thing to do. Especially with a van full of Afghani. I decided to pass through customs as a backpacker with no association to John or Michelle. Thankfully the officials at the other end were more interested in the locals and let us pass.

Once out in the street it took about two minutes to find someone interested in brokering the sale of the cloves. Before long we were weighing up and exchanging a wad of rupees for our precious, but smelly, ten kilo cargo. Money wise it worked out really well.

For the big trip north I sat in the back. John and Michelle were in the front seats. John did all the driving. Mind you he was the only one who could get that old diesel started and artful enough to be able to change its gears. The van turned out to be a terrible tractor-like horror-show that was lucky to ever get out of second gear. It probably could have, but the roads were so bad, and the traffic so thick, that getting a run at 20-30 kilometres an hour was a real treat.

We were also somewhat handicapped in that John had a stash of opium from Colombo that he rubbed into his hash joints on a regular basis. He was very out of it and it was amazing he could drive at all. We followed the main road up from Madras and it took us about a week to travel the 1,600 kilometres to Calcutta (now Kolkata).

At night we would pull over at a trucker's stop which was usually a wide, open parking area surrounded by chai shops. You could get a simple meal and a rope bed to sleep on. It was an open-air affair. John and Michelle slept in the van and locked the door. I slept outside. I wasn't afraid of being robbed. My valuables were in the van and the truckies were Hindus who believed in karma. I slept with one eye open for the first few nights but then had some really enjoyable sleeps in the cool of the night.

The trip up the coast was a non-event. It was really hot. Every now and then we pulled over for a swim in a river or the ocean. One day I dived into a river and scraped my nose on a submerged rock. I was bleeding and realised how infected it might get. I freaked and dosed it with Dettol and put a piece of paper over it to keep the flies off. The paper stuck like glue which meant I had to wear if for about a week before it fell off with the scab. I looked terrible but no one looks sideways in India. There was too much other stuff going on. I paled into insignificance compared to the plight of some of the sadhus, lepers and assorted beggars.

Begging was a profession in India. The skills are handed down in the family. Some children are maimed by their parents so they get more pity and baksheesh. It takes a long time to switch off from these sights but there is nothing you can really do. There are just so many people looking for money. It would be nice to give something that will satisfy the immediate need but it's impossible to break the cycle of dependence.

We arrived in Calcutta late afternoon. You could tell we were getting close as the vehicle and human traffic got so thick we could hardly move. John in his faraway state had no regard for

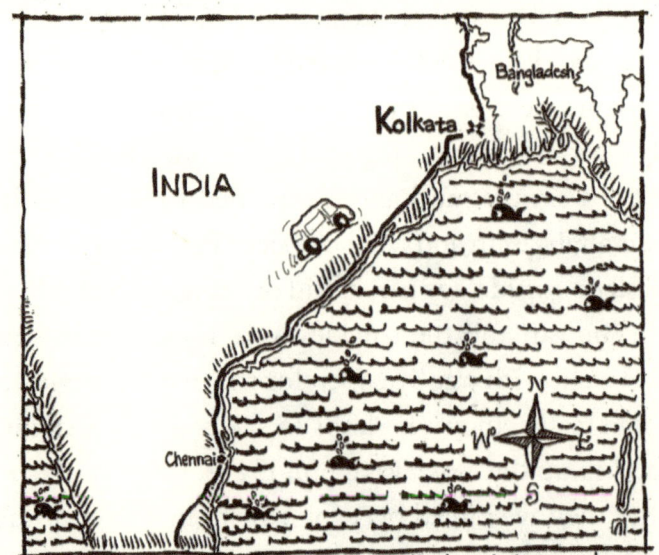

...now for the big trip north... John did all the driving... he had a stash of opium from Columbo that he rubbed into his hash joints from time to time, he was very out of it, and it was a wonder he could drive at all!...

human life and often nudged people and bicycles out of his way. He got a few kicks and thumps on the van from disgruntled people but it didn't deter him. He just pushed his way into the hub and out the other side until we came to a Catholic church compound on the outskirts. He just drove in and set up camp.

The owners didn't say a word so we recuperated there for about three days. There was clean water in the well and it gave us a chance to do some clothes washing. It also gave us a chance to sell off the last bits from my Singapore trip. The guys that bought the watches, the camera and the briefcase stereo were a bit weird. We later figured they were gangsters or cops as the locals were uneasy around them. So given we had other treasures that they might be interested in, we decided to leave quietly one afternoon and we headed north.

CHAPTER NINE

Well It's Alright

We planned to go to Darjeeling and then west through the jungles of Nepal to Kathmandu. It took a few days to get to the foothills of the Himalayas before starting a two thousand metre climb up through the narrow pass. The van moved very slowly but surely. There wasn't a lot of traffic which helped, as we were afraid the clutch would burn out if any stop start work was required. About halfway up it started to get dark. There were no truck stops where we could take refuge so we parked on the side of the road. I got out of the van, rolled out my mat and pulled my sarong over my body to sleep. Normally this was a comfortable enough exercise, but the temperature had dropped significantly and I was chilled to the bone. At about ten pm I couldn't take it anymore. I got up, tried to meditate, and walked around to try and keep warm.

There was little traffic and it was eerily quiet. It was a very long night. I thought about knocking on the van door but John was becoming increasingly tetchy. Almost dangerous. It was the opium - I think he was imagining that the talks I was having with Michelle about his state of mind were romantic chats. I didn't want to be in his face any more than I had to.

I had to keep moving to keep warm so I started walking along the road. The moon was up and I could see where I was going. After about thirty minutes I saw the embers of a fire and figured someone was camped. I started calling out Bom, Bom, Bom Shanka, Bom Shiva, Bom Bholenath. I knew it would be perceived as a friendly call and would give the sleeper a chance to wake up. As I got closer I could see it was a sadhu wrapped in a yellow blanket. He was startled and perhaps thought it was Shiva coming for him. I could see his confusion. This white guy was approaching out of the darkness. I bowed and held my heart and said "Namaste" so he knew I meant no harm. He settled and responded with a "Bom Bom" and gestured for me to sit. He started stoking the fire.

His hair and beard had grown together and matted into a long train that he had wrapped around his waist about half a dozen times to keep warm. It looked like he had a giant snake coiled around him. He started giggling and talking as I tried to explain my car was down the road. I had a small piece of hash in my pocket and offered it to him. He thought it was the second coming. He was so excited and immediately reached for his chillum and mulled the hash into some ganga he had in his pouch. Once he was ready I grabbed a stick from the fire and lit him up. He called out to Shiva as the grass seeds in the chillum exploded … and then he passed it on to me.

We did this about four times as he prattled on in Hindi. I didn't understand a word he was saying but I laughed when he did, and somehow got him to comprehend that I was going to Darjeeling. The hours passed and the fire took the edge off the cold mountain air. Just before dawn I got up, said goodbye, and left with a small piece of burning wood. The heat from the smouldering wood kept me warm until I got back to the van where I got a fire going and sat until John and Michelle emerged for the day.

When we drove past the spot where I had seen the baba the night before. He was gone. I couldn't even see where the fire had been.

That morning we arrived in Darjeeling. What an amazing place. A small trading town perched on the side of a mountain. We sat in a chai shop looking directly across the valley to another mountain range that included Mt. Kanchenjunga, one of the world's highest peaks. The clouds were thick and rolled into the chai shop and out the other side. We enjoyed some of the world's best tea and a couple of coconut oil fried eggs on toast. John put a hash joint together and we enjoyed another cup of tea as the clouds parted to reveal the mountain range in its full glory. It was only a few hundred metres away - just across the valley. It was the same sort of view I had experienced when Olga and I had taken the flight past Everest. As quickly as it appeared, the mountain disappeared again behind the clouds.

The air was cool and crisp so we bought woollen cardigans in the market. We explored the town and the handicrafts shops while researching the onward journey to Sikkim, a small kingdom to the north which had just been opened to tourists. We thought it would be an excellent little side trip but it required a visa, which you could only get in Delhi, so we headed back down the road and on to Kathmandu.

BOM BOM

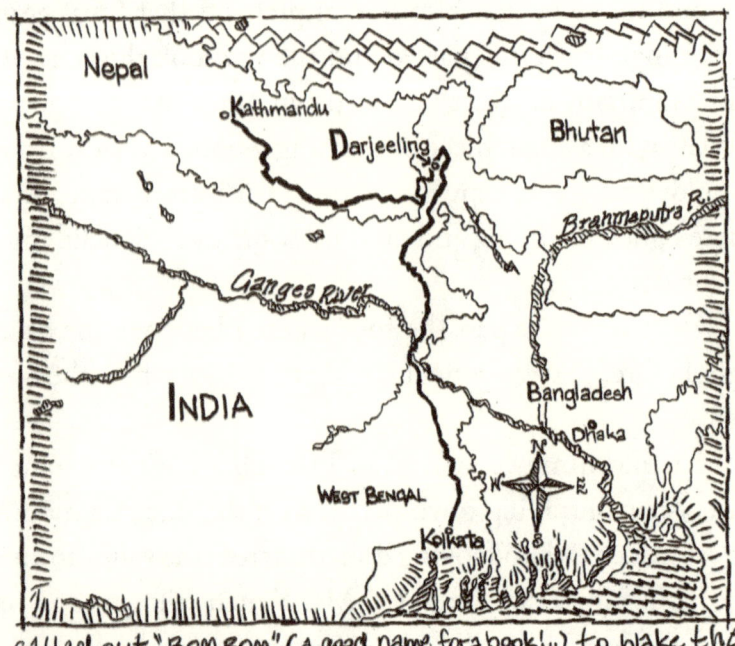

...I called out "BOM BOM" (a good name for a book!...) to wake the sleeping Sadhu....

On our downward journey we crossed into Nepal and picked up the East West highway. It wrapped around the foothills of the Himalayas and passed through some heavily wooded forests. A smattering of farms and timber houses complemented the dramatic landscape. It was beautiful. The van was running like never before. It was in top gear and just gliding. As we descended, the forest became jungle and the road became a slow single lane which had been raised high to avoid flooding. It was mostly tar with a clearing of about ten metres on each side. Beyond that it was jungle. The things that we saw come in and out of the jungle that day were proof of how deep we were.

At one point we saw a log across the road ahead of us, so we slowed (if it was possible to go any slower) and as we got closer

WELL IT'S ALRIGHT

the log appeared to come out from one side of the jungle and go off into the other. As we got closer we realised it was a massive python that was about half a metre thick. John decided it was full steam ahead so he drove what must have been a two tonne vehicle over the top of it. There was a bump, bump and when we looked back the snake started moving to the levy on the right. I have no doubt it was affected in some way but I was not sure who had the biggest fright. It looked big enough to squeeze all three of us out of the van.

After travelling all day we needed to bunker down for the night. Apprehensively I got out and looked for a friendly spot to roll out my mat. I'd been thinking about the sleep out most of the afternoon so I was already in a bit of a state. I kept close to the van and, if I could have, I would have got under it but there just wasn't enough room. The jungle noises seemed to be getting louder and louder. It was a major soundscape of birds and animals. There was the stomping of pigs in the undergrowth. I remembered the snake from earlier in the day and remembered that this was also tiger country. I retreated to the roof of the van and tried to lie in the centre. I wanted to be safe from marauders and I didn't want to fall off. I was awake for the whole night listening to the jungle and praying I wouldn't end up being eaten by something. I couldn't believe the noises of the dawn and then the surprised look from John when he got out to have an early morning piss. I just smiled down at him and said it was the safest place to be and I wasn't doing that again.

That day we made our way into broader valleys and eventually reached medieval Kathmandu. John booked into a camping area and I booked a hotel room. John had been trying to persuade me to travel back to the U.K. with him as a way of sharing the petrol.

BOM BOM

I was having no part of it. Especially after the jungle episode. I was finally free of his OP carry-on and pretty keen to catch up with Hugo. I wished John and Michelle all the best and made my way straight for the American Express office where I asked if they were holding any mail for me. They did and produced a letter from Hugo who I found had left two days earlier and was heading to Australia. Bugger!

According to Hugo's letter Belle had left a month earlier to go back to the States. He was getting lonely and having problems getting his visa renewed. He was secretly hoping to meet up with a girl and go back to Japan but, in the end, he just needed to get to Australia before his money ran out. He asked for my Aussie friends' contact details so he could suss out some work and find out the best place to offload the mountain of clothes he had accumulated. He asked me to write to him at Poste Restante, Singapore which would be his last stop before Oz.

I decided to have a good meal and headed to Freak Street. Before I took a table I went to the art gallery to see Raj who I'd met on my previous visits. He wasn't in but the shop next door sent for him. It was nice to see a familiar face and we smoked chillums into the night. The hunger faded away.

I took a room for a month in the hotel where Olga and I had stayed. I spread my bits around the room and tied my batik-style fabrics to the window spaces. I added my padlock to the door and enjoyed the autumn sun on the veranda. The days were getting shorter and the nights cooler. I was lucky to have this time to have a more detailed look around Kathmandu and its surrounds. I bought myself a yak wool coat to keep warm and was so impressed I bought another for a brother. Raj was a great source of recommendations for good locations to visit so

WELL IT'S ALRIGHT

I saw some beautiful countryside and met some lovely people. I bought some beautiful handicrafts and some rugs to take back home.

Having plenty of time to myself meant that I could get back into some focussed meditation. I realised that I was getting close to leaving so I started thinking about my life back in Sydney and what I might do next. It was really an open book so I figured I should keep calm and see what the lie of the land was when I returned. I was sure it would be all right.

I got a letter from my travelling buddy Hugo. He had arrived safely in Sydney and walked out of the airport with four ounces of Nepalese hash in his Cuban heeled boots. The customs people had told him he was alright and 'just go through'. No bag search or anything. He thought that was very funny. Hugo suggested I go to the shoe shop in front of the dry cleaners in Pig Street and get myself some boots with a hash heel. It was a one-stop shop.

Hugo had received my Singapore letter. He had looked up Pedro and cousin Johnny and was having a great time. He had also connected with a girl who was getting him some shifts in a restaurant. She was as crazy as a cut snake and insanely jealous. He reckoned that he had to keep one eye open while he slept but, to her credit, later on she was able to help him get his Australian citizenship.

As I got close to leaving, Raj asked if I wanted to take some hash home. I thought yes but then no. The next day Raj showed me a plastic satchel about six inches by four inches and half an inch thick. It was hash oil. I hadn't really seen it like this before. He had some in a small bottle which we sampled by dipping a pen knife in and spreading it on the outside of a cigarette. It worked. In a stoned state I said I would have to think about it.

When I caught up with Raj the next day he had four satchels of the stuff. I was in a bit of a predicament. I didn't really want to travel into Australia with a stash. I had travelled everywhere else with my smoko and I believed I had a right to hold enough for personal use but this was pushing the envelope. Australia wasn't like the Asia where most turned a blind eye. It was "rednecksville". I'm sure customs wouldn't have liked me bringing enough smoko to stone all my mates.

If I was to carry it, where would I put it? Hiding it in my luggage would be stupid. I thought about Hugo's boots. Then thought I could put a satchel on top of my foot in each of my shoes. So two satchels. I tried it. They fitted well but I was worried the plastic would burst. That would have been a disaster. The smell would have attracted attention and there was no way you could have got that sticky shit off your shoes, socks or feet. If it broke open on some stage of the journey I would be gone. Raj's idea was to double seal it. I suggested a triple seal.

I am not really sure what I was thinking at the time but later that day I collected two triple-sealed satchels, said goodbye to Raj, and headed back to my room to pack my bags. I was leaving early the next morning. I was anxious and needed something to eat so I hid my stash under the mattress and had a small meal at my favourite restaurant hangout. That night I didn't sleep. I wasn't convinced that carrying it in my shoes was the most secure spot. I was also wondering if I had been set up and whether the cops would be coming in the morning. It was still dark when I got up, had a shower and rethought where I might hide the oil. I tried taping them into my underpants but it was too bulky. So it was back to Plan A.

When it was time, I checked out of the hotel and caught a taxi to the airport. I was glad to shut the taxi door. No tap on the shoulder, thank God. I knew there was no turning back. There was nowhere in those crowded environments where I could dispose of an empty box of matches ... never mind my merchandise. I walked into the airport terminal in Kathmandu, showed my ticket, checked in my luggage which consisted of two carpet bags and two canvas bags full of assorted bits from my trip. I proceeded to immigration and then customs where two officers approached and told me they were going to conduct a frisk search. I stood in the middle of the airport with my hands up while they patted me down and then one grabbed my crutch. I was shocked. Was this normal. Was this the setup I feared? I looked at them and could tell from their faces that it was just routine. They waved me through. I couldn't believe what just happened. What if I had changed my mind earlier that day?

The flight to Bangkok was straight forward. I would change planes and keep flying to Sydney. No real customs process to worry about. After landing I moved to the transit lounge only to find the flight had been cancelled and was rescheduled for the next day. They had organised a hotel in the city as compensation. Not what I wanted to hear. I thought about hanging around in the airport but I didn't like the idea of the airport's intense police presence. I thought it would appear strange if I didn't take up the offer of a free room. Now I had to go through customs with all my luggage and get a bus into the city. Not a good outcome.

Thankfully the customs team were fairly disengaged as it was a forced hotel stopover. I remember getting to my hotel room and trying to dismiss the staff. One was a pretty masseuse and I could have used a good massage but I had to pass on it. Bangkok was not good at that time. Staff would nosey around your room to see what you had. The cleaners would clean everything including the insides of your pockets. I locked the door and took my shoes off. Everything was secure but it did smell a bit. Maybe it was my paranoia but I thought the smell was really obvious. I opened the complimentary soaps and shampoo and peeled the fruit to get some other odours into the room. I had a shower to remove the essence of the day. I really couldn't go out for dinner and leave that stuff in my room as I knew the staff would come into the room to turn down the sheets. I thought about dumping it again but there was nowhere, where I wouldn't be seen or where it wouldn't be found. It hit me that there was no way but ahead.

The next morning I dressed and got the bus back to the airport. This time I had to pull all my stuff out at customs. Luckily it wasn't in my luggage. I remember settling into my Qantas seat with a big sigh of relief because if anything happened now at least I'd be dealing with rednecks and have home support, rather than dealing with crazies in a place far, far away. I tried to act like the other passengers who were returning from their European holidays, but I had a 'Come to Jesus' moment when I looked in the mirror in the toilets. I didn't look like an Aussie returning from London. I looked like a freak. Long hair, moustache, goatee. Thankfully I was dressed in trekker clothing. It was a plausible story that I was coming in from Nepal. Again I thought of offloading the gear but there was nowhere on the plane that wouldn't have caused a ruckus once it was discovered. I tried to tidy myself up, slicked down the hair, and went back to my seat. I put some Tiger Balm on my forehead to get some focus going. At that point we were about an hour out of Sydney so I breathed deeply to calm myself. I knew I had to act normal. If I missed a beat they would be on to me.

On the declaration card I ticked that I had wooden artefacts. I thought it best to declare or all hell would break loose if they found undeclared items. I picked up all my pieces from the baggage carousel and was steered towards two officials. They wanted to inspect my Tibetan wooden dolls and ensure they were bug free. They asked me if I had mud from a farm on my shoes and I said no and showed them the under-soles. They then got me

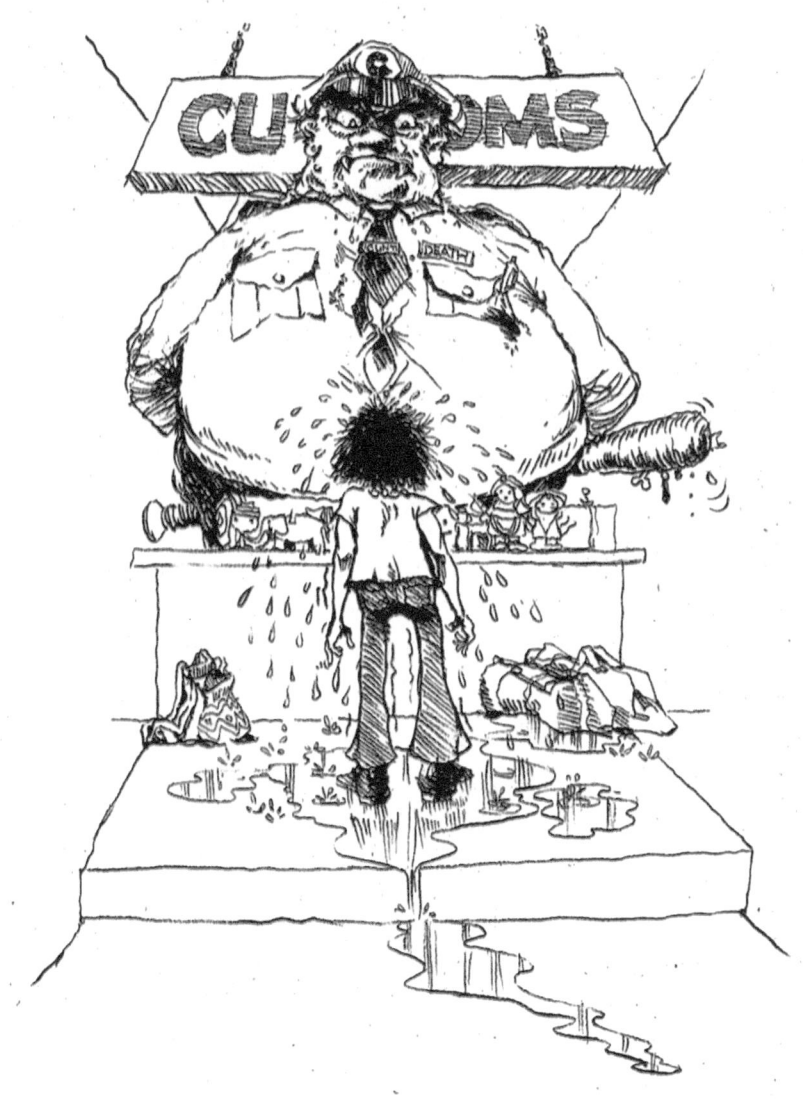

to pull everything out. I had heaps of stuff. They looked intently through it all including having a good look at the empty bags. I tried to tell a story about each item and they looked at me intently as I spoke. They were looking for a chink in the armour. I was thinking "Keep cool, keep cool". There were some long pauses in the conversation and some enquiring looks. I engaged their eyes in a positive way. Then one of them broke the ice and said I should open a shop and told me I could pack it back up and move on. They turned to survey their next interaction. Welcome to Sydney! I thought of Hugo.

I thanked them and moved out into the airport reception hall. There was no one to meet me as I hadn't told anyone I was coming … just in case I didn't come out. I grabbed a taxi and sat in the back. I looked down at my shoes and gave a small grin and a huge sigh of relief.

I was one lucky, stupid boy. Yes, it was just hash oil but the law didn't distinguish and I would definitely have seen the slammer. It would be the last time I would ever put myself through something like that. What an idiot!

Coming back to Australia was just what I needed. A chance to embrace family, friends, work and play. A chance to appreciate just how lucky I was, and a chance to use the smarts of my travelling to a positive end. You'll be happy to know one of the first things I did was buy a motorbike and the latest Stones album *Black and Blue*. The seventies adventure continued.

CHAPTER TEN

He Told Us Not To Blow It

Looking back after all these years, and writing up these adventures, has been a interesting and cathartic exercise. It made me dig deep to remember. The life-defining moments were easy, but with a head full of smoko some of the other events were lost forever. The memories of people I met stayed with me, as they influenced - no changed - my life. It might have been their love and support. It might have been something they said or did. Or it might have been the setting and situation. I learned from them and came back a very different person. I was tested. I came away knowing all about me. My weaknesses, strengths and determination. I felt like I could take on the world. After all I had.

This trip was over. It started on the boat leaving Australia. I was still in a comfortable cocoon at that point. I had friends, structure and civilities. But bit by bit, the further I went, the layers that protected me disappeared. Europe was a personal awakening to the rich history of humanity, the madness of civilisations as they triumphed over one another, and the interdependence of culture. Then there was Istanbul and the crossroads. Two worlds and a bridge between the two and not much more than the ashes of religious aggression. The travelling beyond Istanbul was about the logistics of getting to the next point and the unknowns along the way. They all made the journey and the adventure. And my experiences gave it meaning.

I didn't spend a lot of time in each place, as I had limited money and a destination, and every day had a cost. I suppose this brought out the trader in me. I was always looking for a way to make my money last longer. I was always trying to make extra money to go that little bit further. I think having to be resourceful really shaped my later life.

My Japanese experience can't go unrecognised. How lucky we were to be so low and then get a job and all that money? We dug deep on this adventure. We bared our souls, emotions and bodies. And how interesting to have been exposed to a layer of Japanese society that very few have seen. Thankfully I had a special person to share the intimacies and the head space and we were able to come out the other end of it unscathed.

I saw some amazing things on this trip. The awe-inspiring creations of mankind, the land and sky created by nature, and the unbelievable variety of human beings, all of whom are trying to carve out some sort of existence for themselves and their families. The big eye opener was that ninety nine percent of people no matter what they race or religion were good people. Don't let anyone tell you otherwise. The hardest thing was to accept the situation a lot of these people were in. The politics, poverty and cruelty that they live with had to be put into perspective, and accepted.

I wish I had followed through more seriously on that Anthropology course that Pedro and I signed on to in London to get our Student Cards. I think we would have been a good observers of humankind. As an antidote, the Student Cards were worth their weight in gold. We presented them everywhere and most times they got us a discount, even on the airlines.

The other travellers we came across were also a part of the trip. There were the beautiful souls who had found their way. The seekers on their spiritual path. The adventurers on their way somewhere. The occasional tourist that was way out of place, and the ferals - people who had got down to a basic survival level and just didn't care. Some became wayward because of drugs, or unfortunate circumstances like robbery, jail, religion, or sickness. From time to time I did what I could to help like those boys in Central America and Julia in Pakistan. Other experiences proved it was just best to keep out of their way or you would have become a part of their disaster. Then there were the crazies who really made it hard for themselves by doing shit like riding a horse across Afghanistan or a bicycle from Europe to India. There were those who lived in a cave for six months or indefinitely in a slum in Calcutta. Everyone was out there surviving in their own way. And some didn't make it out, rest their souls!

I was a white bread Aussie with a tight family - a wog when I was growing up and amusingly a skippy to the wogs of today. I was lucky to have had a good upbringing, I had a strong a sense of what was right and wrong. Smoking grass was not a big deal for me. It grew on trees and was put there by nature to fill a need.

There are hundreds of medical and health benefits. Marijuana was good for me. It slowed me down. Gave me time to put things into perspective. It helped me to relax and provided focus when I was being creative or solving problems. Bob Marley once said: *"When you smoke marijuana it reveals you to yourself"*. Wise words.

When I travelled I bought, carried and used weed for my need. I didn't push it on anyone and respected those who felt they didn't need it. There is a lot of hysteria around marijuana and, stupidly, it has resulted in people being jailed, hurt, killed and displaced. I am sorry for them and feel extremely thankful to have escaped the senselessness. Perhaps I was naive, stupid, or a good soul with good karma. Maybe I was just plain lucky. Very lucky.

The world has certainly changed since. The optimism of the seventies has evaporated with hard politics and greed. I feel sorry and sad that my generation saw it coming and despite the protests, rallies and underground media changed very little. The kids today blame the Baby Boomers and they are probably right but I am not sure any generation could have changed what was happening. We did what we could, we spoke up about big politics, big business and the massive greed which has resulted in the rape and pillage of our fragile planet.

Take a look at what is going on today. In the first world most of the people we entrust are corrupt. Power corrupts. They might start out with good intentions but end up with some sense of entitlement, get their noses in the trough, and snort up whatever they can get. In the second and third worlds they are stealing billions, murdering their opposition and killing each other in the name of national security and religion.

Despite a brief period of unity, the Cold War is getting colder. The Wall is down but the Russians are engaged in a subversive war of destabilisation. They don't care so long as they cause chaos and they'll poison, destroy and deny anyone who gets in their way. The Chinese are no better, they are in control and colonialism mode, South America and Africa are constant despot havens. Democracy is in question with its inability to agree on anything, but the freedom and hope it offers the human spirit cannot be overlooked.

Can we all just stop for a second and look around. How could the planet be here for billions of years and man come along and destroy it in a hundred thousand? Nature has provided each of us with a flame of life that is going to burn out after about eighty years … if we are that lucky. As individuals we have a blip. Enjoy the time you have. Create a culture where everyone is helping everyone to enjoy it. Leave the place better than you found it. That should be the price of having a life. Wake up everyone! Humans have a finite time left on this planet. Come together to make it last as long as possible. Trade sanctions, nuclear arsenals, weapons of mass destruction, climate denial and basic human needs must all be addressed.

You might be a North Korean dictator, starving your people, building nukes and asserting yourself as a player. Why? The moment you fire one of those fuckers your entire civilisation will be obliterated along with a big slab of mankind's remaining time on earth. And that was for what purpose? So you can be remembered? As a total dick like Stalin, Hitler, Mao, Amin, Pinochet, Pol Pot and the rest of them?

Putin, I'm calling you out, grow a right testicle and join the civilised world. You might be the richest man on earth, but you are not going to leave any kind of legacy. You have the power and the chance to contribute something to the betterment of mankind. There are one hundred and forty six million of your people wanting. What are you waiting for? Get off your high horse, put a shirt on and really man up!

China, show some respect. There are enough of you living in every society around the world, all contributing to and enjoying the benefits of a universal culture. Why must you demand every one of them surrenders everything to the Party? Why does the party need to rule the earth? Why do your people need to live in fear? If nature had intended that you were to become an army of vacant-brained worker bees then you wouldn't have been born with a brain. Every citizen of China has a brain as well as a heart and a soul. Use this unbelievable resource to help the planet thrive.

America, in God We Trust. Funny to see this printed on their bank notes. Funny too that you need to be a billionaire to become President. Gives you the feeling that they have bought God and their Country off. There are three hundred and thirty one million people in America, surely they can do better. Where are the intelligent, the well-educated, the humanitarians, the visionaries, the orators? Come out and take a big look at the inequality and divisive human rights issues that are currently in play. They are going to come back and bite you big time.

Australia, you're not above reproach. It is criminal how you have sold off the farm and have so little respect for nature and the lucky country. You might not have the fighting power to feel secure but you have the resources to be the food and energy bowl of the world and with this can gain respect and neutrality. Share what you have around. Uncouple your trade dependence on America and China and stop playing politics. Mao once said that Politics was war without bloodshed and War was politics with bloodshed. Be careful what you choose. You've sided with politics on more than one occasion and its ended in disaster.

With the mass movement of displaced people things are going to get very interesting for the whole world. Lucky countries need to provide influence, education and infrastructure. This creates independence and interdependence. Regime change doesn't work - it just leaves a vacuum and civil war. No one wants to leave their home and their culture to live in someone else's society. Trade works. But it can't just be one way.

Our other scourge is drugs, really hard drugs, where it is all motivated by money and no thought of life or social outcomes. How can one be so ruthless that they would mix a bunch of chemicals they know will fuck people up? These guys are murderers. We need stronger border control and heavier penalties to protect us from these ruthless animals. The days of bringing a bit of hash, oil, or grass for friends are gone. Technology has certainly seen to that. The smart thing for governments to do now is legalise cannabis. Imagine how much policing they would save and how much they would make through tax. The kids would be happy, there would be less violence and there would be no need to take chemical concoctions. It might even put the scum out of business. Take note: it's being done in countries around the world and it is working!

Now for the big one - the virus. COVID and the Media. 2020 has seen both outbreaks and they have become a pivot point for the world. Nothing will be the same from here on out. One will take many more lives, millions of jobs and change everyone's way of life. The other will question truth and freedom of speech because of its consolidation and digitisation. As a result of both, governments, financial systems and societies will be re-defined. There will certainly be a lot of legacy debt (not just money) and how we service this is yet to be seen. No, we don't need a good war, because it will be our last. Forget the blame game, we need to come and work together. It's time for the United Nations to step up, have a vision and state it, so we can all line up behind the flag.

I've just looked at the eighty year ruler that is my life, and I'm about to enter the last quarter. The time has definitely come for that small property up in the hills, out of the rat race, away from the plague, Mr. Murdoch's agenda and Social Media. I'm going to grow some herb. The closest thing to god!

Bom! Bom!

The Stoner's Glossary

Acapulco Gold	Mexican marijuana heads renown for their potency and golden colour.
Acid	LSD (Lysergic acid diethyl amide), a non addictive hallucinogenic drug. Effects include altered thoughts, feelings and awareness. Made popular by Timothy Leary in the sixties to promote mind expansion and truthfulness.
Amsterdam Putty	hydroponic marijuana pollen that is kneaded into a putty and smoked with tobacco.
Bhung	not very potent marijuana leaf and seeds, crushed and boiled down in a flavoured buffalo milk drink to provide a mild high.
Bidis	cheap cigarettes. Indian tobacco flakes hand rolled in a tendu leaf and tied off with a piece of colourful string. The leaf is often flavoured with fruit.
Blotter	blotting paper that has been soaked in LSD. Small pieces are cut and sucked to get high.
Bom Bom	Awake! Awake! The call to Hindu god Shiva when lighting a chillum.

Bong	simple water pipe, usually bamboo. Marijuana is loaded into and burnt in a "shot" or "cap" bowl.
Buddha Sticks	highly potent marijuana grown in Thailand, Cambodia, Laos and Vietnam (The Golden Triangle). The heads are stripped from the stalk and tied with thread around a bamboo skewer about six inches long.
Charas	hashish made from the pollen of live marijuana plants.
Chasing the Dragon	inhaling the smoke from smouldering opium.
Chillum	conical pipe used to smoke marijuana and hashish.
Choof	marijuana or tobacco.
Choofing	smoking.
Ciggies	cigarettes.
Coke	cocaine.
Dope	any form of drug. Most commonly referring to marijuana.
Ganga	Indian name for marijuana.
Gold Tops	gold colour mushrooms with psilocybin delivering an intense psychedelic experience.
Grass	marijuana.
H	heroin, an opioid, injected or smoked for pain relief and euphoria.

Hash/Hashish	resin of marijuana pollen compressed into a putty that when heated burns. Usually sold in kilo, one hundred gram and ten gram (Tola) pieces.
Head	a person who is a stoner but more likely someone who trips.
Heads	marijuana seed pods/flower buds.
Herb	marijuana.
Hubble Bubble	middle eastern water pipe.
Jay	joint.
Joint	marijuana rolled with cigarette papers.
Kif	marijuana that is rubbed through a cheese cloth to get a fine powder.
Marching Powder	cocaine.
Marijuana	plant containing cannabis sativa ingredient delivering a "high" when smoked.
Mary Jane	marijuana.
Mr Asia	international drug syndicate.
Mull	marijuana mix used in a bong.
Mullumbimby Gold	best marijuana from this regional New South Wales town.
Mushies	psychedelic "magic" mushrooms.
Na Naas	your brain. "Off your na naas" is to be stoned.

Opium/OP	poppy seed pod bleeds a latex that can be smoked or processed into heroin and morphine.
Panama Red	red coloured marijuana from Panama.
Primo	first or top grade.
Roach	remnants of a joint that can be lit and smoked if held in a roach clip.
Rollie	roll your own with cigarette papers.
Scoobie	a joint.
Shisha	a hooka pipe. Available in Arab cafes, and often shared in a group.
Smack	heroin.
"Special"	food or drink that has been infused with marijuana.
Spliff	Jamaican style multi cigarette-paper joint. Can be 4-6 papers in size. Or a rolled newspaper if you have that many friends.
Stoke Up	light up a joint, a chillum or bong.
Stoned	under the influence of marijuana.
Tabs	tablets of LSD.
Thai sticks	Buddha sticks from Thailand.
Trips	LSD experiences.
Wacked	get high very quickly and very intensely.
Zombi	marijuana and euphoria.

About the Author

Vientiane 1976

Mark A Tesoriero spent the next forty five years working in advertising and production. He was a pioneer in the digital media space and built many of Australia's first websites, CDROM zines and streaming video events. He has ghost written training books, produced TV and radio, and executive produced the film thriller, Bad Bush. He is now writing to clear his head of his unique adventures with the next instalment the story of advertising in the eighties. He still hangs out with Pedro and Hugo.

Truth is often stranger than fiction and sometimes worth sharing. Thanks for reading. If you enjoyed Bom Bom, please let your friends know and leave a review on Good Reads. Life's too short. Be Happy.

www.ingramcontent.com/pod-product-compliance
Lightning Source LLC
Chambersburg PA
CBHW021945290426
44108CB00012B/972